Praise for *Inspire Your Career*

"Inspire Your Career is about motivating yourself to reach your greatest professional potential. If you're looking for a competitive edge in the workplace, it's a must read."
— Michelle DiEmanuele, President and CEO Credit Valley Hospital

"Inspire Your Career is a valuable tool in providing knowledge and insight to our national treasure - our youth. *Inspire Your Career* does a great job of providing much needed perspective and balance for our next generation leaders."
— Ross W. Maund, President and CEO, Junior Achievement of Canada

"Patricia Barbato explains, in a refreshingly honest way, the lessons she has learned throughout her career. The chapters are brimming with valuable no-nonsense information and advice."
— Irene Lewis, President and CEO, Southern Alberta Institute of Technology

"So many young people enter the workforce without a realistic understanding of what it's like. This book gives young professionals or recent graduates the tools and practical information they need to understand and fit into the reality of today's workplace." — Lauren Friese, Founder, Talent Egg

"Inspire Your Career tackles the key career related issues that everyone will experience. Patricia's practical examples and advice make the book a must read for everyone embarking on a successful career."
— Darren Jack, Co Founder, Impact 360

"Inspire Your Career has great tips on finding and using mentors to accelerate your career."
— John Carbrey, Founder, Intrafinity and creator of MentorMatch software

"I needed this book when I started my career in that first coop placement. *Inspire Your Career* is perfect for people new to the workplace."
— Andre Edelbrock, CEO, Ethoca

"Patricia has really hit the nail on the head for those just entering the workforce or for anyone wanting to make a difference in their career. The book delivers advice in a practical, fun-to-read manner."
— Rich Patterson, Owner, Patterson Brands & Ninepointten Media

"This is a book you won't want to skip a sentence or jump a paragraph. I wish this book was around when I was first starting out in my career."
— Cathie Brow, Senior Vice President, Revera Inc.

inspire your career

Strategies for Success in Your First Years at Work

Patricia Barbato

INSOMNIAC PRESS

Library and Archives Canada Cataloguing in Publication

Barbato, Patricia, 1964-
        Inspire your career : strategies for success in
        your first years at work / Patricia Barbato.

ISBN 978-1-897178-92-8

        1. Success in business. 2. Happiness. I. Title.

HF5386.B2296 2010   650.1   C2010-900663-1

The publisher gratefully acknowledges the support of the Department
of Canadian Heritage through the Book Publishing Industry Development Program.

Printed and bound in Canada

Insomniac Press
520 Princess Ave., London, Ontario, Canada, N6B 2B8
www.insomniacpress.com

This book is dedicated to my big, beautiful, lively Italian family.
You enrich my life every day.

Foreword

When I was matched with my "Big Sister" Patricia back in 1988, I was ten years old. I never imagined how important her mentorship would be in my life, beginning as a child and continuing now through my adult years. I learned first-hand how a person's positive influence can make remarkable things possible. Although you may not have Patricia as a mentor in your life, you have this book, which is infused with her knowledge, practical advice and, most importantly, her natural inspiration.

Patricia Barbato shows how any one of us can transform our career, our workplace, and everyone in it. She freely shares her own personal journey as an employee, a manager, and leader for organizations and boards. After reading this book we are forced to look at our careers through a different set of eyes—seeing with an open perspective filled with possibility. Each chapter, paragraph, and sentence that you read will ring true because it may have happened to you. If it has not, it will. *Inspire Your Career* is full of helpful tips and sage advice on how to handle your job and workplace in a positive way.

The information in this book is valuable to you and each person you pass it on to. The reflection questions allow you to silently sit back and consider your answers. You will learn more about yourself, which is a pathway to personal fulfillment. You will learn how to use your natural wisdom to better assess a situation and decide how to proceed.

Patricia always strives for greatness and helps others see their greatness too. Whenever I encounter her colleagues, they share stories of the impact she has made. They always express deep appreciation and gratitude for her inspiration. Inspiration strengthens companies and energizes attitudes and behaviours.

This book will have a profound effect on the way you do business and the way your career evolves. We can learn to lead and influence in a way that positively affects our surroundings and others.

Knowing my "Big Sister," that is her goal. She wants you to read this book, and influence every person you can, so that we can all learn from each other and make this world a beautiful place.

Patricia and I spent the twentieth anniversary of our mentoring match in the sacred land of Machu Picchu in Peru. Like the Incas, I encourage you to plant the seeds of your career purposefully; tend to them and nurture them. May you and your career reach new heights and make quantum leaps. You will be the change that this world needs because it starts with you. Good luck with your future harvest. Inspire your career!

Keesha Rosario
Managing Director, SMART Watering Systems
Vancouver, Canada

Contents

Introduction

I have been very fortunate to enjoy a rewarding and successful career. Much of this success is a result of taking on responsibility at a very young age, which I did largely through necessity. I grew up with my extended family and was the eldest of 12 children living in the same house. Most of the adults spoke little or no English. I remember being as young as eight years old and navigating various government agencies trying to find answers for questions that the adults had. I started working for my dad when I was 12-years-old doing payroll for the construction company that he owned with my uncles. I loved working and thus was fortunate to acquire a lot of skills very early in life: skills that helped me accelerate in my career. By the time I was 30, I was a partner in a public accounting firm, chair of the board for a charity that works with children, and teaching at a local college. Ten years later, I was the president and chief executive officer of a healthcare organization. This book is based on my personal experience at work and in life, and the wisdom and knowledge of others whom I have worked with over the years: my colleagues, my bosses, and my staff.

Why did I write this book? The answer starts with my passion for mentoring. Once I attained more senior positions in my career, I wanted to find a way to encourage people, especially women, to pursue leadership positions. I began facilitating group mentoring sessions with young people to discuss career-related issues. These small groups gathered in the evening, in my home, and were largely organized through word of mouth. In the process of providing these interactive sessions, it became clear that the majority of questions were from people who were in the formative stages of their careers. The topics these participants wanted to explore ranged from dealing with conflict to networking techniques. After years of conducting these mentoring sessions, it seemed necessary to articulate and share the questions and wisdom that emerged from the discussions. This book was written to help anyone who wants a more successful, fulfilling career. I have had the privilege of mentoring hundreds of wonderful people through work relationships, teaching environments, and the mentoring sessions described above. The inspiration for this book comes from the inquisitiveness, desire to learn, and candour of these remarkable individuals.

Inspire Your Career focuses on providing insight and practical advice for the most common issues faced by those early in their career path. Much of the available business and career material on the market is focused on topics that are meaningful when searching for a career or for those already well into their careers. This book fills a void for those learning what is involved in being part of a workplace. It is applicable to any sector, industry, or profession. *Inspire Your Career* is also organized as a reference book, so that you can reread specific sections that become more relevant as you advance in your career or when a particular situation arises. In addition, Chapters 8 through 11 are geared to first-time leaders who are taking on roles as managers, supervisors, or team leaders. These chapters are also relevant if you aspire to become a leader and they are useful to understanding what a manager might be looking for from you. You will also see the icon ⓘ throughout the book. This logo means go to my website at *www.inspireyourcareer.com* to download a free worksheet or access additional resources on the topic being discussed. Check it out.

This book can be summarized into three key messages:

1) **Have a great attitude.** Everyone appreciates people who are positive and have a can-do attitude. Be engaged and take pride in your work.

2) **Learn to self-reflect.** There are opportunities everywhere to learn more about who you are so that you can become the "best" you. Learn to be open, to listen, and to have the courage to change.

3) **Build great relationships.** Learn to cultivate positive working relationships with everyone you interact with. You never know when or how or who will be able to help you in the future (or when you can pay that forward).

This book was written with three intentions for you. The first is that the practical advice and tips contained in this book help you to reach your greatest career potential. Your career is one of your biggest assets and has an effect on all aspects of your life. Your career is like a tree, grounding you in security and financial support, allowing you to branch out to new and exciting areas or destinations, and providing you with the fruits of gratification and achievement. In this book, we'll talk about transitioning from school to a work environment, building a network, how to orient yourself in a new job, how to deal with common workplace frustrations, finding mentors, and much more. I hope that you are able to both succeed and be truly happy in your career.

The second intention of the book is to encourage you to help your workplace reach its greatest potential. A recurring theme, and the most important message in this book, is to develop your self-awareness. Self-awareness is the key to unlocking your potential, and it allows you to bring out the best in yourself and those around you. I encourage you to be curious and courageous about looking deeply into who you are. This book is filled with opportunities to self-reflect. Take the time to complete the reflection exercises and think about your answers. By raising your own awareness you can be the inspiration for creating a healthy, positive, and dignified workplace. Mahatma Gandhi's words, "You must be the change you want to see in the world," are entirely appropriate in a work setting. You must be the change you want to see in your workplace. By changing the pattern of negative energy and by using yourself as the vehicle to turn things around, you actually fuel a new pattern, a new way of thinking, and a new way of doing things. People are attracted to this, they emulate it, and it becomes contagious. Everyone has the power to positively change their environment if they start from a place of honesty, compassion, and desire to be of benefit to others. You can cultivate this skill and positively influence the environment in your workplace. We will explore your role in knowing your blind spots, dealing with conflict, and taking a lead in inspiring a better workplace.

Finally, the third intention is that you, together with others like you, become the catalyst that evolves businesses, organizational structures, and the environment in which people work. We need a seismic shift in what "business" means and a new paradigm to create the foundation for finding solutions to the world's problems. Most of the structures currently in place within organizations are a product of the past: command and control-style authority, thick hierarchy, and confusing bureaucracy. We are in a new place now and it is time to shed these systems. The problem is that most people in charge right now may not want to make these changes and likely do not know how. You will have the answers. Many readers of this book will be young, extremely fluent in technology, and adept at large-scale collaboration. Albert Einstein said, "No problem can be solved from the same level of consciousness that created it." You are the new consciousness. I urge you to take your place in creating new organizational structures and workplace environments that move us forward by quantum leaps. This book is a starting place for helping you become the kind of leader who can create this level of change.

My deep and sincere aspiration for you is that you become an authentic, inspiring leader, positively influencing your environment, your community, and your world. I am confident that you have this potential, and confident that you can make a tremendous difference. The world needs your unique perspective, your energy, and your gifts. I urge you to open your mind and your heart and unleash your greatest potential.

Chapter 1
Getting Started

"Envision your dream—Focus your intention—
Invite the universe to participate."
Unknown Author

Every career starts somewhere: a first big break, help from a friend or family member, a co-op job that becomes permanent, or a lot of dogged perseverance. We can all remember the day we got our first "real" job. And while it is great to get a job, it is never too early (or too late) to be thinking about your career. What do you want to accomplish? Where would you like to be in five or ten years? Ultimately, you are responsible for your career path. You are the only one who can identify your interests and unique talents and how you would like to best use them in your career. And while your career may take some twists and turns, the decisions you make now will determine your future, including your earning potential, how satisfied you are in your job, and what you will accomplish.

Have a Plan and Be Opportunistic

One thing is certain, if you do not know where you are going, you are definitely not going to get there. You may be incredibly organized, already have a clear plan in mind, know where you want to be, how to get there, and what you would like to accomplish in life. That's great! There will also be those who have absolutely no idea and have not given their career much thought at all. Instead, they have decided to wait for opportunities to present themselves. The best approach is to both have a plan and be completely open to opportunities that present themselves. This means having a sense of where you want to be in the future, while staying alert for opportunities that cross your path. Approaching your career in this manner is like starting off on adventurous road trip. You have a map of where your ultimate destination is and some of the stops you would like to make along the way, but you are completely open to changing routes or exiting to pursue something that looks interesting.

A career plan is essential to create a blueprint for your future. Since most of your adult life will be spent at work, isn't it worth some thought and realistic planning? Your choices over the next few years are critical and will have a significant impact on your lifestyle and the level of gratification you can expect from your career. Developing a plan may be easy for some who have a clear and precise idea of what they would like to do. For others, this will take some effort. You need to think about what your strengths are, what kind of activities make you happy, what you are passionate about, and what gifts you think you have to offer. It may also be helpful to be clear about what you do not want to do. Answering these questions requires serious self-reflection and is best done when your mind is clear and open. You may want to speak to people who know you well and ask them, "What do you think I would be good at?" or "What do you think my strengths are?"

Reflection Exercise
What do I like to do?

What am I good at?

Visualize yourself in the future. For example, pretend you are at your 50th birthday party: Where are you? What are you doing? Where have you travelled? What will you have accomplished? Are you happy? Make a commitment now to write down your goals, aspirations, and dreams. These may not all be work related, but you never know what will happen. There is always the possibility of a convergence of work related objectives with other more personal goals. In fact, it would probably be ideal to have the things you are passionate about be part of your work. Write down everything you think of—all your goals, aspirations, and the things you would like to do in life, even if they sound far-fetched or too ambitious. Aim high and listen to your innate wisdom.

You should also identify any steps that might be necessary in order to accomplish the goals; for example, if you want to start your own business, this may require financing, research, etc. You can also write down a time frame for what you want to accomplish. You could set out what you would like to accomplish by an actual year, or perhaps by the time you reach a certain age. A written career plan is a summary of *what* you want to accomplish in your life, *when* you want to accomplish your goals, *how* you can accomplish your goals, and *who* can help. A written career plan will change over time, but spending time now, thoughtfully considering where you want to be and what you want to do will help you organize your thoughts and give you an opportunity to consider your future. Here's a template of what a career and life plan might look like:

Goal	By when?	Skills/ Resources I need	People who can help	Questions I have
Own a business	35 yrs old	Funding/ business plan	Parents/ Friend of family	Who can I learn from?
Travel to Africa	Before my 30th birthday	Time off/$ for trip	Aunt/ Teacher	Go with a group?

ⓘ *www.inspireyourcareer.com*

This written plan is now a starting point and a reference that will help guide you. Refer to these goals frequently to remind yourself of what you said you wanted to do, to check on how you are doing, and to adjust your course as required. Over time, your priorities will change and shifts in your thinking will occur. Some things will come off your list and others will be added.

Another important reason to have a career plan is that it can help to guide you in the future when you are considering a career transition. Any time that a new opportunity arises, you can go back and look at your plan. Does the opportunity help you achieve your goals? Is it aligned with what you want? When you sense the need to change jobs and find something new, you can review your plan. The notes you make now of what you want to accomplish in your life can be a way to measure whether future choices are aligned to your plan. For example, someone who you worked for in the past has started his own company and wants you to join him. His new company offers you an opportunity for building the business from scratch and profit sharing. You are not that happy in your current job and this opportunity looks great. Go back to your plan. It may say: "Be an entrepreneur" or "Be part of a start-up," which would align very well with the opportunity in front of you. However, if your original plan includes "Oversee hundreds of people," or "Always be financially stable," you have a warning to look at the opportunity more closely. This should prompt you to ask more detailed questions about the new job opportunity such as: Can I deal with the risk of a start-up? Can I live with not having people report to me? You may still decide to take the opportunity, but your own goals can serve as an internal guiding system to help you make the best choices for yourself.

Shift from School Mentality to Work Reality

There are things in life that we don't appreciate until they are gone. The time and freedom we have while going to school are good examples. While in school, the world revolves around you. You are often the focus of your parents' energy, attention, and funding. You meet many different people, have an active social life, and are able to spend your time as you desire. You can make spontaneous decisions, change courses, change professors, change academic majors, and play sports: you have a lot of freedom. Once you join the workforce, there are many adjustments to be made. You have to go to work, be on time, look professional, and follow the workplace routines. Your parents may now expect you to be independent, responsible, and self-supporting. It is not as easy to coordinate time with friends, or participate in all the activities in which you used to be involved. You have to plan and request time off for vacation and may be required to work long hours or on weekends. You will probably start with a meagre two weeks' annual vacation allowance, which can seem impossible to manage. Your workplace will also have a pre-established culture that won't be familiar to you when you first start. For example, a workplace culture may be very quiet and subdued or it may be very loud and busy. It will take time to understand the culture of your new work environment.

How can you make the transition from school to work smoother? First of all, just recognizing that it is a significant transitional period in your life will help. Be in tune with how you are feeling and recognize that much of this relates to the changes in your social circles and daily activities. You are in the process of change. You are shedding certain routines, beliefs and assumptions and acquiring new ones.

I remember when I started my first job. I wanted to scream! I felt like a white laboratory mouse being asked to do the same boring thing in the same boring place. It was painful, especially coming straight out of the very social, freedom-filled school environment. It was hard to be in the same small cubicle, all day long. It was difficult to work with so many people when I was used to working independently. It was challenging to get out of the "cram for exams" mentality. I now needed to actually retain information, remember where things were, and what was outstanding. Be patient with yourself, and appreciate that a work environment is very different from your school environment. Over time, you will adjust and, with perseverance, you will succeed.

Another transition common with those coming out of school will happen within you. You will be redefining who you are. This can sometimes be difficult. You may have had a certain identity at school; perhaps you were the organizer, the jock, the partier, the studious one, the councillor, the social convenor, or the workaholic. Perhaps you became very passionate about something at school: the school itself, a certain sport, a social cause, or your department. Once you leave school, your old identity disappears because the context is gone. In your new work environment, the context is entirely different and likely very different from what you were accustomed to at school. You will need to redefine yourself in a new context. This takes time and an appreciation that you are ending one phase of your life and entering a new phase.

An area that can cause a great deal of consternation is friendships.

You probably met and had regular contact with numerous people while in school; there was a large network of friends and acquaintances that were part of your life. Once you start working, trying to maintain a large network of friends is futile. Most people who leave school disperse to various cities, jobs, and futures. You may find yourself starting to let go of certain friendships from your life. This is a natural, but potentially painful process, as you start to discern the value of your friendships. Ultimately, it serves you best to create a positive environment around yourself that facilitates your growth and development. In this transition from school to work life, you start to develop and decide what the meaningful relationships in your life are and will be. During this phase, be really honest, both with yourself and with others. This is another opportunity in your life to reflect on who is important and what is meaningful to you.

Pay Off Your Debts

If you are in debt after finishing school, it is important to pay off all your loans as quickly as possible. When you are fresh out of school, you likely do not have a lot of other major financial priorities, such as children or a mortgage. It is an excellent time to try to keep the same standard of living that you had in school so that you can keep your costs low and pay down as much as possible on your debts. Set a goal for yourself of how soon you would like to pay everyone back, even if it is a five- or ten-year plan. Create a budget for yourself that itemizes how much money is coming in monthly and then subtract the monthly costs that are fixed (rent, car lease, your debt payment, etc.). This tells you how much is left for discretionary things like entertainment or clothes. Do not spend above your means. Invest in your future by delaying extraneous spending. Try to make your monthly debt principal payment as high as possible, so that your debts and loans are paid off as quickly as possible. The time to start is right now.

It is very tempting, especially once you start earning a steady paycheque, to want to buy new things. If you allow yourself to buy everything you think you deserve, it won't take long for that paycheque to disappear. When you are just out of school, no one expects you to drive a fancy car or have a beautiful condo or wear expensive clothes; all this will come in time. Focus your efforts on having a clean financial slate for the future. Reducing your debt as quickly as possible will give you much more flexibility and choice in the future. If you are debt-free, it is easier to travel, to start a business, or start saving for a house. My youngest sister recently made her last payment on her student loans, which included substantial debt from both an undergraduate and law degree. She emailed the whole family exclaiming, "My money is now my own!!!" It's true, paying off your debt will give you a huge sense of accomplishment and start you off on a great financial footing for the future.

Finding a Job

Finding a job, particularly when you are first out of school, can be challenging. Many external factors will influence your search. For example, if the economy is poor, you may find it difficult and more time consuming to find a job because so many qualified applicants are available and competing for fewer job positions. If the economy is good, you may find a job, but it may not be exactly in the area or at the income level that you were hoping for. If the economy is great, you may find yourself in demand in many places. Notwithstanding the external environment, there are still a number of basic ways that you can increase your success at finding a job including:

- Advertise Yourself—Tell everyone you know that you are looking for a job, in case something comes up in their workplace or they hear of something. Be able to succinctly articulate the kind of work you are looking for.
- Find Door Openers—Ask family and friends to connect you to people in their networks. You will still have to "close the deal" if an opportunity arises, but it is a huge help if the door to an opportunity is opened for you.
- Be Creative—Consider how you can find and meet with specific people who you would like to work for. Find ways to get noticed such as writing an article, organizing a seminar, or posting your work online. Use professional networking sites as appropriate.

- Persevere —Looking for a job can be a lot of work. Commit to spending the time and energy that is needed. Don't get discouraged by setbacks; start fresh every day with the determination to find a job.
- Be Open-Minded—There are many jobs that may not fit your initial criteria but that could provide experience and an opportunity to develop skills. In some ways, there is no "wrong door" to starting your career. All learning will be valuable to you.

(i) *www.inspireyourcareer.com*

Consider Entrepreneurship

One of the great benefits of being an entrepreneur is that you become the captain of your ship by charting the course of where to go next. It can be a rewarding, exhilarating experience. It is also not for the faint of heart; being an entrepreneur means taking risks, not having the structure associated with most workplaces, and constantly thinking ahead about the next customer and sale. I met a young woman recently who started a career website right after graduating from university. Starting a business soon after you graduate can often be easier than trying to do it later in life. There may be government programs or incentives to assist you in starting your business. There are non-profit groups and associations that may be able to lend expertise, mentorship, or support. You likely do not have the responsibility associated with a mortgage or family. You are likely able to borrow from people and places to get you started. For example, you may be able to use a family member or friend's space for your new business and avoid paying rent. You can work at keeping your overhead low in order to put as much effort as possible into your business model. The young entrepreneur I mentioned feels that starting a business right after school, with so little experience, is an advantage, because you do not know what you don't know. This open state of mind fuels innovation and encourages entrepreneurs to reach out to others.

One aspect to keep in mind if you choose entrepreneurship is that you will have to take charge of your growth and development. Since you are not working in a structure with built-in learning opportunities or education and training, you will need to seek this out. This may take many forms, including speaking to other entrepreneurs and business people, getting linked in with a support group, finding a mentor, or joining an association affiliated with the product or service you provide. You need to find the time to continue to advance your business acumen, people skills, and sales skills. Since you do not have a boss, you can reach out to your customers to ask how you can do things better, what is working, what is not, and what advice they have for you. Stay open to learning as much as possible as you work on making your new business a success.

Project a Professional Image

Understanding how you project yourself is important to understand, both prior to starting a job (at interviews for example) and when you start your job. A series of experiments by Princeton psychologists Janine Willis and Alexander Todorov reveal that all it takes is a tenth of a second to form an impression of a stranger from their face.[1] Researchers in another study found that personality is manifested through appearance and observers use this information to form accurate judgments for a variety of traits. This means that your appearance matters and that it quickly forms the basis of others' opinion of you.

Your image, which includes your attitude, how you carry yourself, how you dress and how you speak, sends a message to everyone around you: your colleagues, your boss, and your clients. Your image reflects a sense of harmony with your body and a connection to the world. At minimum, try to be conscious of the image you are projecting. Does it reflect who you are and how you want to be perceived? For example, your attitude not only says something about who you are, but also has a direct impact on the people around you. If you have a negative, pessimistic attitude, not only does it affect you and how you view and interpret the world, it also affects everyone you come into contact with. What kind of attitude do you have? If the woman beside you had your attitude, would you like her? Try to look at yourself objectively to discover what kind of attitude you are portraying in the workplace. Then ask yourself if it is appropriate and would be appreciated by others. As a manager, I have written people off in the first few minutes of their job interview based on attitude alone. Attitude is what will be reflected to clients and what has an impact on a work culture. You are in control of your attitude and your attitude is a powerful influence on how others perceive you at work. Choose a positive attitude every day.

Reflection Exercise

What kind of attitude do I project on a daily basis?

_____

_____

_____

What kind of attitude do I want to project?

_____

_____

_____

The way you carry yourself is full of subtle meaning. Do you hold yourself upright and walk purposefully? Do you move slowly and thoughtfully? Are you sloppy? Do you portray a sense of confidence? We assess people almost immediately upon meeting them, even if they have not spoken. I once worked for a very successful partner in a national accounting firm. She had started with the firm in her 20s and became partner by the time she was 30. I remember what her assistant said about her, "She acted like a partner from the day she walked in here." Obviously to become a partner she would have needed the requisite skills and experience; however, the conscious image portrayed by the young woman right at the start of her career only helped her chances of becoming a partner. Confidence begets confidence. When you are confident about who you are and what you want, it gives others confidence in you. Does the way you carry yourself at work portray where you want to be?

In addition, your work patterns and choices create an image for others of who you are. Based on your interaction with others, how do you think they perceive you? For example, what do you email your coworkers? Consider what you are forwarding them, the content of your emails, and the tone of your communication. Ask yourself if it is appropriate in the workplace. How do you respond to requests for assistance? Are you open and engaged or are you a barrier to others? Consider how you deal with stress. Do you make scenes at work, thereby affecting everyone around you? Do you complain and vent at every opportunity? Do you become closed and inaccessible to others? People will quickly determine whether you are considerate of others in your work area. For example, do you clean up after yourself in the staff kitchen? Do you keep personal phone calls, which can be overheard by others, to a minimum? Do you use an appropriate tone and volume when you are speaking on the phone? Be mindful and appreciative of how your actions and attitude directly affect others and thus their opinion and perception of you.

The way you dress carries a message about you too. It has a connection to dignity and grace. I had a wonderful friend in her 90s, Rae. She grew up in an era where you dressed up when you went to visit someone. She hated jeans, and hated how young people wore jeans everywhere. I usually visited Rae on Saturdays and it would never fail; I would get into my car, start the engine, and then realize I was wearing jeans. Back in I went to change. It would really have bothered Rae if I visited her wearing jeans. Dressing is a sign of respect toward yourself, others, and a sign of respect for the situation you're in. You create a certain kind of energy by looking groomed and appropriately dressed. This does not mean you need to spend a fortune on clothes or start wearing blue suits every day. We can ensure our clothes are clean, tidy, and that we are appropriately dressed. Always be yourself, but be thoughtful about how you dress. If you are unsure, consider what situations you will be in at work and who you will be meeting. It is also a good idea to be aware of any company dress codes or policies. If in doubt, ask your boss. Remember, how you dress sends a clear message to others. Always carry yourself in a professional, appropriate way.

Another important part of your image is your speech. Be conscious of the words that you use, how you use them, and seek opportunities to listen instead of speak. The workplace is not an appropriate environment for swearing, vulgarity, inappropriate jokes, or condescending language. There are a lot of opportunities to have fun and laugh at work, but speech that is disrespectful will harm the atmosphere of the workplace. Speech should always be respectful, even in situations that are highly charged, whether positively or negatively. If you are ever in doubt, ask yourself "Would I say this to my mom?" or "Would I want someone to speak to me this way?" Use your own judgment to discover and discern how to speak in a way that is respectful and will engage your audience.

Negotiate your Pay

Negotiating your pay is an important aspect of getting started in your career and becomes increasingly important as you move up. In some situations, negotiating your pay may be very difficult or impossible. For example, if your role is one within a unionized environment and you are part of the bargaining unit, your pay and the related benefits will be dictated by the existing union agreement. There will be very little, if any, room to individually negotiate pay or other benefits. Likewise, if your position is part of a non-unionized environment, but is essentially identical to other positions, a pay scale and salary grid will likely exist for that position, and therefore dictate the remuneration that you will receive. You may have some room to manoeuvre if you are with a smaller organization and/or your role is unique. Another factor that will greatly influence your ability to negotiate is the economic and/or financial climate. This may have an influence, either positively or negatively, on the company and the entire sector.

When you do have an opportunity to negotiate, it is a good idea to think through exactly what you are looking for and to try to rank your wish list between "must have," "nice to have," and "not essential." This will help you understand which items you feel most strongly about and keep you focused when you enter negotiations. Consider your total rewards, both remunerative areas, such as base pay, bonus, profit sharing, pension, as well as other benefits such as number of vacation days, ability to work from home, whether the company provides a cell phone, or flexible hours. Before you start a job is the time to negotiate the best offer. The company has decided that they want to hire you, and now they just have to finalize the remuneration. You will never have a stronger negotiating position.

Going into negotiations with an open mind and a clear idea of what you would like to achieve will help you navigate through the process. It does not have to be a win-lose proposition. Take your cues from the employer as to when to start the negotiating process. Usually it begins after the last interview where you are told you are the preferred candidate. Once an offer has been made to you, take time to prepare a counter offer, one that is reasonable in the circumstances. Be as informed as possible by trying to find out rates of pay for comparable positions. You can also ask working colleagues their pay ranges and what benefits they receive. The negotiation process may occur verbally or the employer may request that you provide your counter-offer in writing. Work collaboratively, respectfully, and with the intention of coming to a fair and equitable agreement.

Which Do You Choose?

You are the preferred candidate. You:
a) Take whatever pay is offered.
b) Ask for a car, eight weeks of vacation, and three times more pay.
c) Counter with a 10% increase in pay, a company cell phone, and one more week of vacation.

If you are a woman, you may not negotiate as often or as well as your male counterparts. Research in Linda Babcock and Sara Laschever's book *Women Don't Ask: Negotiation and the Gender Divide*, reveals that men are significantly more likely than women to use negotiation to advance their own interest, whether it is a pay increase or promotion. Generally, men have a more confident attitude about what they are worth, or they have a more aggressive approach in trying to maximize their remuneration. Women, on the other hand, tend to take what is offered and do not use the opportunity to negotiate. This exacerbates the existing salary differential between men and women for equal work. Based on this research, female readers may need to work harder to negotiate a fair deal. This may include overcoming obstacles that are stopping them from effectively negotiating with their employer, whether fear of rejection, fear of looking too aggressive, or fear of leaving a bad impression. While both men and women need to negotiate the best deal they can, as a woman, you need to put more effort into making this happen.

Build a Network

Building a network is like buying property in Monopoly. With every new contact acquired, you increase your value and your potential to receive dividends in the future. Your network may be the source of your next job opportunity; it may include future clients, or be a way to find a service or skill you need. Your network starts with the people you know now and your network will grow as you come into contact with others in the future. These contacts can be from both inside and outside your work environment. Trust your instincts about people who you like or with whom you resonate immediately. Do not be afraid to ask for their contact information and ask if you can stay in touch with them. It is never too early to start building your network. Accumulating a list of contacts that you can use in the future is one of the most valuable resources in your career.

Starting to build your network is easy: just start with who you know right now. This might include current or past work colleagues, people from school, friends and family, as well as acquaintances from social or other groups. It may surprise you that many of your closest family members and friends do not know exactly what you do. There is some networking required even with this close group. Take opportunities to succinctly describe where you work and what you do. Think about meeting an important person in an elevator. You have a few minutes at most, what would you say? What is your 20-second "elevator pitch"? Sharing your story and your goals allows others an opportunity to help you now or in the future. Remember that many of the contacts you have right now will be in completely different places in five or ten years. Your peers and friends may become entrepreneurs, company presidents, or leaders in their field. You never know what can happen in life, so be mindful and respectful of the relationships that you have. "Never burn bridges" is a great rule to live by. Keep your contacts in an organized fashion, making sure that you have as much contact information as possible. As your network grows, organizing contacts into groups is a good idea so you can better track people. You may want to note when and where you met them in order to jog your memory later when you are seeking something from your network. As you move through your career, collect the contact information of new people you meet, and add them to your network.

Reflection Exercise

List the names of three people you know right now who could help you with your career.

_____

_____

_____

How will you reach out to each person for advice, assistance, or counsel (e.g. meet to get advice, ask the person to connect you to two other people)?

_____

_____

_____

_____

_____

You can proactively seek out opportunities to build your network contacts by participating in internal committees or working groups, which might expose you to people from outside your department. You can participate in external committees, such as those related to your industry, sector, or profession. You can attend industry, sector, or professional events, such as conferences or trade shows. You can use social networking sites, participate in development courses, or volunteer with an agency or charity. Another important way to build your network is to ask people you know if they know someone you should meet. This is a useful approach when you are job searching, but is also helpful when you are seeking advice or guidance in a particular area. All of these are great ways to meet people, often people who you would not otherwise be exposed to. If you are attending a networking event, be prepared. Ensure you know what your objectives are in attending the event: Is it to meet people in a similar role? Find new clients for your business? Meet a potential employer? Whatever your objectives, you should have a clear idea of what you are trying to accomplish and tailor key messages aligned to your objectives. For example, if you are looking for more clients for your part-time business, you need to be prepared with a short message of who you are and what your company does. You need to have business cards and/or promotional material ready to hand out. You want to be purposeful and prepared for opportunities to expand your network. In any networking opportunity, asking others to tell you about themselves is a great way to open up a conversation. Everyone has a story to tell and drawing this out will establish rapport and become the launching pad for a good relationship.

Building your network also requires you to nurture the relationships that are important to maintain. Throughout your career, you should identify the individuals who you need to stay in touch with, whether due to their status, their experience, their connections, or their link to your current role. Consider how to best maintain a good relationship. You may want to send an annual holiday card, birthday greeting, or periodically meet with key contacts. There is definitely a need to be proactive and conscious about maintaining and nurturing relationships. For example, if you have a past boss who you really enjoyed working with, you may want to stay in touch by communicating every few months about what you are up to or perhaps ask the person for advice over lunch. That person's career will grow in the future and you will continue to have a good resource for advice, counsel, and, possibly, future job opportunities. In order to be effective in building your network, you need to reciprocate and be effective for others. Take opportunities to "give forward" by listening and being supportive to those who reach out to you. Being authentic and proactive will go a long way in establishing and nurturing your relationships with people who could be very important to you in the future.

Inspire Your Career Tips

- Write down your career and life goals and work towards them.
- Stay open to career opportunities that might arise.
- Pay off your school loans as quickly as possible.
- Create a professional image.
- Make an effort to meet new people and build your network.
- Nurture important relationships.

CHAPTER 2
Boss Bliss

"He who is not a good servant will not be a good master."
Plato

You've started a new job. You are excited and looking forward to the challenge. You likely met your boss through the recruitment process, so you have some sense of what she or he is like. The ensuing relationship will be the most influential factor affecting your overall work experience. It will determine if you are happy in your job, how much you learn in your role and, ultimately, whether you stay with the organization or not. Thus, the relationship with your immediate boss is pivotal—for both of you. One thing that is easy to overlook is that the relationship is two-way. You are looking for a challenge, for a chance to prove yourself, and for opportunities to learn and grow. Your boss also has a lot at stake. Your boss has hired you believing that you are the right person for the job; that you will deliver on the expectations that have been set, that you will fit in with the team; and that you will be an asset to the organization. Your boss's success also relies on you. The energy, attitude, and perspective that you bring to the relationship with your boss will have a direct impact on how much you get out of it.

Stay Cool

The way that everyone starts a new job is different. If you are a new professional who begins immediately working with clients (for example a teacher, nurse) you will probably feel like you've just been thrown to the wolves. No amount of school will have prepared you for how busy and stressful it can be when you first start your job. If you are starting in a company, you may be overwhelmed by the number of people you meet on your first day and what seems to be a labyrinth of an office. Your boss may be nowhere to be found and not part of your orientation process. Alternatively, you may have an excellent orientation and your boss may be right there beside you. You might meet some really odd characters when you first start or you might meet some wonderful people who are incredibly helpful to you. You may have arrived on your first day of work, eager and keen, only to discover that there is no cubicle for you, no computer, and your email address and business cards are not ready. After your first day, you might feel exhilarated and energized or entirely depressed and wondering if you made the right career choice. Stay cool.

The learning curve when you are starting your career, and even when you are starting a new job, is steep. The learning curve is not just about the actual job you are doing, but it is also about the work dynamics, the office politics, the culture, the hidden assumptions, the acronyms being tossed around, the people you work with, the clients you work for, and the list goes on. It really does take time to sort out all of the subtleties of how everything fits together and where you fit within the work environment. Be patient with yourself and be patient with others; you have a wonderful opportunity to learn and grow. You're new, so you can ask a lot of questions. Ask anyone and everyone about everything. Ask about the specific things, like "How do I order business cards?" and "Where do I find letter head?" as well as the intangible things, like "What is it like working here?" and "Who should I get to know?"

Which Do You Choose?

You start a new job. You:
a) Demand to know how your boss is going to make your job interesting and challenging.
b) Zealously try to prove yourself every day.
c) Balance being keen and setting goals with observing and learning.

A bit of humility is also helpful when you first start a new job. There is a need to respect the history and complexity of the organization you have just started working for. Your colleagues will appreciate you being respectful and giving them some reverence for being there longer. Even if you have a hundred ideas after your first week, it's probably a good idea to keep them to yourself for a little while longer. In your first weeks, try to listen and use appreciative inquiry, for example, "I am just curious, why do we do things that way?" Try to keep a good balance between proving yourself as an individual and being seen as a part of the team. Your boss is looking for a balance of initiative and conformity—a balance of being a strong team player and excelling in your own right. You absolutely have a lot to offer, but when you first start, pick your opportunities with thoughtfulness and care.

Orient Yourself

Orientation has two elements: orientation to the organization and orientation to your boss. Most organizations will have some kind of formal orientation process in place. This may or may not be adequate. Do not hesitate to undertake additional orientation tasks so that you can get familiar with the organization and the sector or industry that you are in. For example, take the initiative to review the internal and external websites, research your competitors, read your annual report, review any data or performance indicators that are public, and review internal organizational communication and policies. Approach your boss to further support your orientation by providing specific documents for your review, such as your department's financial information or annual goals. You may also want to speak to others within the organization. Ask your boss whether it is appropriate to speak to colleagues, other departments, or to clients to better understand the current state. Depending on your role, it may be appropriate to ask for a plant/office/site tour. The best time to research and learn more about the organization is during the first week and before you get busy with other tasks.

The other element of orientation is to familiarize yourself with your boss's style and expectations. It is important to understand how your boss operates and what her expectations are, so that you can maximize your efforts and create a stress-free environment. By matching or mirroring your boss's style, you will be able to ensure that a strong working relationship is formed. The best way to do this is by both observing and asking questions. For example, you may notice that your boss is very organized and likes to have agendas and minutes for meetings well ahead of time. If you take a role in one of the meetings, it is important for you to do the same thing; that is, send the agenda and minutes well in advance. If you are working on a project or conducting some research for your boss, ask how he would like your results presented back. If you do not, you might deliver an award-winning briefing note, which your boss disregards because he prefers to hear results and talk things through. Another great way to orient yourself to your boss's style is to ask others who work for, or with, your boss. Ask your peers what they think you need to know about your boss—does your boss have any particular patterns or pet peeves? Understanding your boss's style and expectations will help ensure that information flows well between the two of you and that progress is happening in a mutually acceptable way. Regular interaction is also important in order to make sure that the two of you stay in sync. Ask your boss if you can set up regular meeting times together to review jobs, status reports, concerns, etc.

Understand your Boss's Goals

If you do not understand what your boss is focused on, it is easy to do things incorrectly. You may think that something is important, but it is really of secondary importance because of a different and more urgent deadline that your boss has to meet. You want to understand her priorities so that you are aligned in meeting overall objectives and you can see how your work aligns itself with what your boss is doing. Make sure that you periodically sit down with your boss and ask, "What goals are you trying to achieve?" and "What are your priorities right now?" Understanding why your boss needs something will also give you important insight. For example, you are asked to complete a project. By asking the questions above, you may find that your project will be used for a presentation your boss is making to a senior executive. By understanding the priority of this project from your boss's perspective, you are able to give this project, which has significant importance, the attention and focus that is required. If your boss is not as accessible, you can attend organizational information sessions, read newsletters, your organization's intranet, or other communication to keep abreast of what is going on within the organization. You can ask for a copy of the strategic plan, which is the organization's written description of its future state. The strategic plan outlines the vision for the organization and the steps it will undertake to achieve that vision. You can also request information on departmental goals and budgets. This information might be confidential, but you won't know unless you ask. Depending on your organization, there may also be public, external benchmarks to meet, such as a certain occupancy level or an industry ranking. Benchmarks are the standards or the comparison from which the performance of an organization is measured. Get a copy of any external benchmarks or data and be familiar with how your organization is doing.

Having regular communication with your boss and checking in on priorities will help you stay on top of what is important and help you to set your own goals. Once you have oriented yourself within the organization and you feel you have some sense of its priorities, develop your own list of objectives that link to your boss's and the organizational goals. Share your goals with your boss to make sure that they are aligned. You can also keep a running list of tasks and projects that you are working on for your boss, so that it is easy to communicate and discuss the status of each item, bring up any issues, and ask questions. Remember, your boss can help remove roadblocks and barriers for you if you can clearly communicate.

Take the time to discover the optimal method of communicating with your boss. Does your boss prefer getting email from you? Does your boss have an open-door policy and prefer you to drop in? Does your boss prefer a more formal face-to-face meeting that is scheduled in advance? Find the best way to communicate with your boss so that you have a regular exchange of information.

Do Not Assume

You know the saying about assume? Well, it's true. The scenarios are all too common: people assume that their boss knew how busy they were, what they had on their plate or that they were struggling with priorities. The mirror image also plays out, where the boss feels the employee should have known that something was critical or should have known the deadline. We can't read minds. Your boss can't read your mind, and you can't read hers. I remember being mad at one of my bosses for weeks because I believed she had created a barrier to my project. I discovered later it had nothing to do with her. I had spent all kinds of time feeling anger towards her and allowing the stress to build in me. All this for nothing; it was a misunderstanding that could have been cleared up if I had only asked for clarification. It is a mutual responsibility to communicate. Instead of sitting at your desk silently cursing your boss because you have too much to do and feel overwhelmed, ask yourself if your boss actually knows this or if you are assuming that your boss knows. Have you spoken to her about prioritizing your work? Have you asked for help? Think about the assumptions that you are making.

When you receive a work project, make a commitment that you will not assume. Try repeating back instructions so that you are sure that you understand what you are to do. Ask clear, specific questions in order to avoid going down the wrong track or spending a lot of time on something that is not needed. For example, if your boss gives you a research project to do, you could ask "How would you like me to present the results? Would you like a list of each site I search and the findings in each? Or would you prefer only the top ten that have the most information related to the topic? Would you like me to print relevant sections from the sites?" These questions will help ensure that both you and your boss have the same expectations in terms of what you are supposed to be doing. It is also helpful to check in periodically, again, so that you do not go off course or find out later that there was a much easier way to do something. Initiative is fantastic, but spending hours of time on something that in the end you have to do over again, or worse, that your boss has to redo, will not make either of you very happy. You want to work smarter, not harder to accomplish your work. I once worked for two days on endless spreadsheet scenarios, thinking I was doing exactly what my boss wanted. It wasn't at all what he wanted. This can definitely happen to you. It is best to acknowledge what happened, learn from the experience, and move forward.

Reflection Exercise

List three mistakes you have made at work.

What did you learn from your mistakes?

_____

_____

_____

Be Patient

It is very easy to feel a sense of entitlement at work. You may feel that you deserve to be noticed, that your viewpoint is really insightful, that your boss should recognize you more, that you should be promoted sooner, or that you should be making more money. Most people are always looking for the express lane and trying to get "there" faster. Your assessment of your skills and potential, while possibly accurate, may not be aligned with what your boss sees in you. It is really important to practice patience in your job. It can take time for your boss to develop an opinion of what your strengths are. He needs to see you demonstrate your skills over time and on a consistent basis. So the fact that you think you are good at your job will only be acknowledged when your actions, decisions, and work really show your skills, and these are demonstrated over and over again. Completing one assignment well will not signal to your boss that you should be promoted. He will only see one good assignment. Excellence is not a one-hit wonder. Excellence needs to be a habit, which takes time to demonstrate. It may take the tenth or twentieth good assignment before your boss starts to form an opinion of your performance.

The other area of patience relates to your actual work assignments. While we may envision ourselves doing tremendously challenging and important work, our job is always filled with routine, mundane tasks. This is as true for a front-line worker as it is for a president of a Fortune 500 company. Not everything you are asked to do will be exciting and challenging. Even as the president and chief executive officer (CEO) of a company, I had to organize my expense report and review time sheets; these were unremarkable tasks, but ones that had to be done. Some aspects of your role will involve dull, repetitive, or tedious tasks. Be patient with the work you are receiving and take things in stride. Have a good attitude about your role and be willing to do a wide range of tasks.

The Frustrations

There will always be frustrations with your boss and, more broadly, with your job. If you let these get to you, if you internalize, magnify, or dwell on them, they are going to grow out of proportion and your mind will indeed make a mountain out of every molehill. Soon you will feel so deeply negative and stressed that it will be difficult to see any possibility of improvement. In most cases, there is something we can do with our outlook to create a positive impact on the situation. Even if your boss truly is a dreadful person, you can affect your interactions. If nothing else, you can seek neutrality in your dealings with your boss, so that a negative interaction does not affect your attitude or performance. The key is to find the courage to put your ego and fear aside to clearly see what is going on. Look for alternatives, solutions, and workarounds so that you can maintain a balanced attitude and still get your work done.

There are many frustrations that are common, regardless of where you work or what position you have. These frustrations do not distinguish between the front line and the president; they can and will happen throughout your career. Be aware of these common issues so you can handle them in the best way possible. Here are five common frustrations, along with a few suggestions for dealing with each one:

Frustration #1: I don't have time

This frustration happens frequently. There never seems to be enough time to finish our work, be with our clients, or speak to our team members. There is a constant feeling of urgency in everything we do.

Solutions:

Prioritize

Seek clarification of what is a priority, at the onset and along the way. Communicate with your boss, to understand the priorities and timelines. Ask if anything does not need to be done, or what can be delayed.

Automate

Look for manual processes in your work routine that can be automated. Be conversant in technology that can assist you in your role.

Ask for help
Ask your boss for assistance e.g. a summer student, an agency temp, temporary reassignment of another person. Ask if there is a more efficient way of doing your task/project.

Improve your process
Look for wasted time or duplication; eliminate any waste or steps that do not add value to the process/project. Speak to your boss if improving a process requires resources beyond your role or department.

Shadow someone who's more efficient than you
Ask to job shadow someone in a similar role, who seems to be able to keep up with the workload; seek to learn new ways of doing things.

Frustration #2: I don't have the information or knowledge
You may realize at the beginning of a task, or partway through your work, that you do not have the required information or knowledge to complete what you were asked to do.

Solutions:
Ask where to get the information or knowledge
Do more research, ask colleagues, be inquisitive about seeking out the information or knowledge

Ask how to approach the issue
The work you have may seem impossible for you to do, but you may not be seeing it correctly. Ask your boss or colleagues how to work with the situation you have.

Do not panic
Dive in, do your best, and learn from the experience. Most of us have to deal with issues when we have imperfect or incomplete information and limited time. Learning to make good decisions in such circumstances is a skill that can be developed. If you are given

an opportunity to do your best in a situation where you do not have all the information and insufficient time, do not be afraid of it. It is an opportunity for growth and development.

Frustration #3: I don't have the resources

This comes up in many situations and the resources may be physical in nature (e.g. computer hardware, software), financial (e.g. a larger budget), relate to human resources (e.g. need to hire another team member), or relate to needing more time. This is a difficult area to either resolve quickly or easily, due to multiple approvals required in most organizations to increase resources. This is a common frustration for people at all levels.

Solutions:
Ask if there is any room in the budget for what you need
You won't know if you do not ask. Your boss may have some room in the budget to purchase the new software, ergonomic chair, or social activity you want to organize.

Find a creative alternative
If there is no room in the budget, consider how you can still accomplish your goal. Perhaps you can charge a fee for the social activity or find free software that is comparable to the one that you want.

Borrow or barter from others
Another department or team may have what you need. Consider borrowing resources from other areas or barter one resource for another.

Frustration #4: How was I supposed to know?

This common frustration erupts when a person is questioned about something she or he did or did not do. Your boss may approach you asking why something was done a certain way, or why you neglected to do a particular task. How do you avoid not knowing?

Solutions:
Ask clear, specific questions
Do not walk away from your boss unless you are crystal clear about

what is being asked of you. Always ask what the deadline is for any task or project. Ask if you should speak to anyone else or if there is anything else you should know.

Anticipate who or what will be affected
Always consider who or what will be affected by what you are doing. For example, if you are being asked to compile a report, make sure you understand whom it is going to and how they are going to use it. This helps to guide how your work should be done.

Anticipate the consequences
Think ahead to what happens next. You email something important and get an out of office reply. That means the person did not receive the information. Think ahead to what that means; what are the consequences? What do you need to do?
If you make a mistake, consider if there are remedial actions that can be taken. Take note of what you have learned from making the mistake.

Frustration #5: I'm waiting for a decision or more information
This frustration is fairly common in our increasingly interconnected world. Your work stops because you are waiting for either a decision from someone on all or some aspect of your work or you are waiting for information from another source within the organization. Because you have a deadline, the lack of timeliness of others' decisions or information has a direct impact on you.

Solutions:
Communicate why and when you need the decision/ information
Others you are relying on may not know the effect that they are having on your work. Explain why you need the decision or information and how this affects the project or task you are working on.

Ask if you can do anything to help
Go to the person or department from which you are waiting for a decision or information and ask if there is anything that you can do to assist in the decision being made or the information becoming available.

Ask for an update
You may need to ask for updates on the decision or information on a regular basis. You want to balance this with an appreciation for what the other person is working on.

Start a different project
If you have communicated to your boss why there is a delay in completing your work, start into another project.

Which do you choose?

You need information from a colleague and the deadline you set is long gone. You:
a) Complain to your boss about the person's incompetence.
b) Don't say anything, but hold a grudge.
c) Approach the person and ask if there is anything you can do to help him get the information to you.

Frustrations in a work environment are inevitable. They will always occur. What you have direct control over is how you deal with the situations as they arise. Try to be open-minded, resourceful, and have a sense of humour about what is happening.

Appreciate the Bigger Picture

At some point, your boss will make a decision you do not like, implement something in a way you do not agree with, or constrain one of your brilliant ideas. There is a power and authority differential here and you are not in the driver's seat. Your boss has pressures and constraints that you are either unaware or only peripherally aware of. Even if you do not understand or agree with a decision that's been made, you need to accept it and move on. This is an important point. Prior to a decision being made, it is great to provide feedback and input, but once it is made, you need to support it. This does not mean support it and grumble about it for months afterwards to anyone who will listen. It means support it and do your best to make it work. If it really is a bad decision, your boss will soon figure that out. Remember, your boss is human, just like you. Your boss is going to make mistakes, including making a bad decision or giving you bad advice. Even if you do not like everything about your boss, you can still appreciate and respect that she or he is your boss. There is always something to learn from people in your workplace, particularly from the person you report to, even if it is how *not* to do things.

Which do you choose?

You're not crazy about your boss. You:
a) *Complain to anyone who will listen.*
b) *Put in only enough effort to get by.*
c) *Quit.*
d) *Stay respectful and seek to learn the skills and knowledge your boss does have.*

Remember that your boss is working within a larger context than you are and is making decisions based on an assessment of the "bigger" picture. Try to put yourself in his shoes. This is particularly useful when you are trying to get, sell, or present something to your boss. You want to focus and demonstrate the benefits to the department, team, or organization as a whole, versus the benefits to you. Try to incorporate the bigger picture into your analysis so that you can present the benefits, risks, and costs, along with your ideas, in a balanced, comprehensive way.

Take Initiative in Your Performance Review

Everyone feels some level of anxiety before a performance review. There is the worry about what will be said about you. Often there is a missed opportunity in taking the time in advance to consider what you want out of the review. A performance review is a two-way exchange and is a fantastic opportunity to better understand what you are good at and in what areas you can improve. Be prepared to listen to what is presented to you. You may be surprised by something that is said— simply acknowledge it. During your review is not the time to argue about it; you will need time to digest what has been said and really process the information. If, during the review, you do not feel that you understand something, ask for examples or clarification. For example, if you are told that people do not feel they can rely on you, ask for further explanation or concrete examples. Does it mean you take too long to respond to requests? Does it mean people do not feel you are honest? Does it mean you do not meet deadlines? This is the time to get as much feedback as you possibly can. Most importantly, you want concrete suggestions and ideas on how you can improve your performance.

This is also the best time to bring up issues with your boss, areas of concern you have, ideas, and any special requests such as a new project you want to be involved in or your desire to change your hours on Wednesdays. Carefully think through, in advance, whatever it is that you are looking for. You want to approach your boss with a positive attitude and have answers for any concerns or questions. For example, before you request a change to your hours on Wednesdays, find out in advance if your organization has a policy on this, or if any precedent has been established through your personnel department. Present how you will make up the hours and how you feel this small accommodation will make a big difference to your work-life balance. Consider if there are certain skills you would like to develop or training that you would like to take, or if you want to join a committee or taskforce. This is also a great time to discuss how things are going from a communication and workflow perspective. You can ask if you are meeting your boss's expectations and if there is anything she would like to see you do differently. Spend the time in advance thinking about what areas you want to discuss with your boss. It is also important to start a list of your accomplishments or results and update it on an annual basis. This list is an excellent document to provide to your boss during a review.

Suppose you have asked your boss for extra training or you have identified that you would like to be on a committee. Your boss may not immediately respond to your request. You have planted a seed, but it might take months before an appropriate opportunity to act on your request is available. Your boss may be juggling multiple priorities and also needs to consider equity amongst the team, so your request may not be able to be accommodated immediately. The important thing is that your boss is aware of what you want and you have clearly articulated your request or objective. This is an important starting point in moulding your career.

If a review is not scheduled, or your organization is not rigorous in managing this process, ask your boss for a formal meeting to discuss how you are doing. It is easy to shy away from this exchange, but talking about your performance is one of the most important conversations that you can have at work. Your personnel department may also be helpful in providing you with advice on how to initiate a performance review process with your boss. If you work in an environment where performance reviews are not conducted, for example, you work in a family business or started your own, you can seek input from key stakeholders. This may include key clients or vendors. Anyone who works with you on a regular basis could be asked to provide input on how you are doing (peer review), and asked for advice on how to do things better.

(i) *www.inspireyourcareer.com*

Make Your Boss Look Good

It is easy to forget when you are busy and have a project that you think is really urgent, that your boss also has a lot to do. Your boss is managing multiple relationships with direct reports, his own boss, colleagues, and external stakeholders. Each of those relationships comes with certain expectations and needs. Your job is to help deliver on the results that your boss is accountable for. If you help your boss achieve his objectives, you too will be successful. This does not mean you shouldn't push back or express your concern over issues; however, your boss is your link to the rest of the organization, to resources, to people, to projects, and possibly, to your next job. The day may come when you are asking your boss to be a reference. The way you interact with your boss now will dictate what kind of reference you are going to get in the future. Even in situations where you do not like your boss, you can still be respectful and try to make things easier for both of you. Invest yourself in trying to make your boss look good in front of staff, senior executives, and, especially, his boss. The best way to do this is through results and performance. Delivering on objectives, projects or work makes your boss look good. Praising your boss in front of him and or others, without substance to the praise, will not take you far. Be motivated to create a win-win situation for your boss, you, and the company.

Inspire Your Career Tips

- Starting a job can be overwhelming—stay cool.
- Understand your boss's style.
- If you're not sure—ask.
- Be solution-oriented when faced with frustrations.
- Put yourself in your boss's shoes.
- Use your performance review to learn more about yourself.

CHAPTER 3
Know Your Blind Spots

*"Courage is what it takes to stand up and speak; courage is also
what it takes to sit and listen."*
Sir Winston Churchill

Have you ever wondered how someone could not see her faults?
It is so obvious to you that she is arrogant, critical, a perfectionist,
needy, inconsiderate, talkative, or aggressive. How could the person
be so completely oblivious to what seems to you to be habitual, obvious patterns of behaviour? Well, what if we all had these elements
of our personality or style that are not that pretty, or inappropriate
patterns of behaviour that seem totally obvious to others? Yes, you
too may have certain behaviours that others see very clearly, but
that are blind spots to you. The question is, do you have the courage
to recognize, reflect, and act on what you learn about yourself?

Blind Spots Revealed

According to Merriam-Webster's dictionary, a blind spot is "an
area in which one fails to exercise judgment or discrimination."
You can think about it in terms of driving a car: blind spots are
places where your side mirror cannot reflect what is there. For example, if a bicycle pulls up beside your car, it may be in your blind
spot. Even though the bicycle is actually there, you can't see it. For
our discussion, blind spots will be aspects of who we are that we
cannot see clearly. Blind spots develop out of fear. We are afraid
to lose control. We are afraid to be vulnerable. We are afraid to be
"found out," and that our inadequacies will be open for all to see.
We are afraid of the invisible enemies who might disrupt our world,
our values, or our belief systems. The fear takes root in our mind
and holds on tightly, not wanting to let go. When a situation arises
and our fear creates a response, we consider the situation and our
response to be integrated, as if the response flows logically from

the situation. If my colleague is tapping his pencil incessantly on his desk and I yell "Stop doing that!", it is easy to view the tapping and my response as being integrated. My response flows from the situation that my colleague created. Therefore, there is a natural sense of justification in my reaction. I believe that my reaction to the situation was appropriate. In reality, the situation (the pencil tapping) and my response (yelling) are separate and distinct. One does not flow from the other. I have *chosen* my reaction to the situation. When we automatically or unconsciously link a situation to our response to it, the sense of justification is inherently there. In our simple example of the tapping pencil, the situation seems inflexible and closed to me. I feel that there is nothing left to do but yell at my colleague. When we feel that a situation is inflexible and closed, the words and actions that follow are also inflexible and closed.

I once worked for someone who was overbearing and loud. I hated being on an assignment with him. I visualized him as an ogre, eating live children for breakfast and destroying everything he came into contact with. Let's take a look at what was going through my mind. I had made a judgment that his personality was offensive. The resentment had taken root in my mind and was holding on tightly giving rise to the constant vision of him as an ogre. So if this was going on in my mind, how do you think I treated him? You got it—horribly. Even though I tried to be nice, I am sure my disdain was palpable every time we were together. And if this is the energy I was projecting toward him, what could I have possibly expected in return? And so this poisonous dance kept playing itself out, over and over again, day after day at work. Did it cause stress? Absolutely. My relationship with him seemed suffocating and closed. I could not imagine, and clearly was not open to, any positive resolution of our relationship.

One day, at a company social event, I saw the ogre with his family: a lovely wife and two children. He was not doing anything particularly unusual, he was just there and interacting with his family while enjoying the afternoon in a park. I remember thinking he seemed like a great dad and that he had a really nice family. In that moment, my mind's clenched grip on my judgment let go. The ogre dissolved and I saw him with fresh eyes. I saw him as another human being. This small break, this ray of openness, is the key to greater self-awareness.

There is a word in Japanese pronounced "ma," and it translates roughly as "the space between." By separating a situation from your reaction, you can create "ma." And in that moment of "ma" you can tap into something truly powerful: the opportunity to make a different choice. In the previous pencil tapping example, I couldn't see any space between my colleague's behaviour and my reaction to it. If I could, I might have made a different choice. I might have been able to use humour to diffuse the situation or I might have had more patience and avoided yelling. In that space between the situation and your reaction, you have an opportunity to change your behaviour and break patterns.

Little by little, when you start to see the sharp contrast between what your mind thinks is happening and the pureness of what is really there, untouched by judgment or fear, you have tapped into greater self-awareness. By harnessing your ability to become more self-aware, you can reach your fullest potential. Stanford's Graduate School of Business Advisory Council was asked to recommend the most important capability for leaders to develop. Their nearly unanimous answer was self-awareness.[2] How do we develop self-awareness? How do we get to know our blind spots? We will discuss a three-fold process of seeing yourself, understanding what you learn, and acting in a new way.

See Yourself

In order to know yourself, you first have to be willing to see yourself for who you really are—faults and all. If you are not willing to see yourself, then you are the person we discussed earlier, the person about whom everyone is thinking, "Wow, can't they see that about themselves?" To begin to know yourself you must have the intention of wanting to see and to be more self-aware. This is not as easy as it sounds. Many of our patterns have been built up over years. They may be connected to childhood experiences, to our culture, our religion, a traumatic event, or a particular relationship. With such a long and deep history, it is no surprise that we are deeply attached to our judgments and fears. They are comforting. Losing them is terrifying. If you can accept that this is a challenging process, but an incredibly worthwhile one, then commit to better "seeing" yourself.

There are a number of ways to better understand who you are at work. The first thing you can do is ask for feedback. This feedback could come from your boss, either through your performance review or periodically as opportunities present themselves. During a performance review, if areas of development are not identified, ask for that feedback. If an area of development has been identified, make sure that you really understand what is being said. If it isn't clear to you, ask your boss for specific examples or more explanation.

About ten years ago, I received a performance review, which, while generally positive, had a statement that stunned me. The comments on the review stated that several people who I worked with were intimidated by me and afraid to speak to me. I was honestly shocked—talk about a blind spot! My instant reaction was to deny the feedback and blame the people who made the comments. My shock and instant reaction to the comments really made an impression on me. I truly did not see this about myself, even though it was very clear to others around me. Having this information and "seeing" this about my personality took me down a long journey of self-discovery. I wanted to be a strong leader, but not the kind who people were afraid of or intimidated by. Recognizing my blind spot helped me make the conscious decision to change. I wanted to be a better person. Seeing that part of myself changed my career.

Which do you choose?

You receive feedback that you are not a good listener. You:
a) Discount the person who provided the feedback.
b) Get angry.
c) Mull it over. Pay closer attention to yourself and consider how to improve your listening skills.

If your workplace is not committed to conducting regular performance reviews, you can ask your boss for one, or at least ask for feedback after a project is complete or after a meeting where your boss has seen you interact with others. You can solicit feedback from your colleagues, or other appropriate people, like the chair of a committee you are on. Ask open-ended questions like, "Do you have any suggestions on how I can improve my communication?" or "How do you think I could be better at work?" You can also ask your friends or family members for feedback. While they won't necessarily have seen you in a work environment, habits and patterns that you have at work will tend to flow into your private life. Ask them, "If there is one thing you could change about me, what would it be?" or "Is there anything about me that bothers you?"

Another opportunity to see yourself more clearly is after a particular situation occurs that leaves you feeling uneasy, troubled, or highly emotionally charged. The situation itself and your reaction to it hold valuable information about you. Think about the last time you were really upset with someone. Ask yourself why you were upset. What can you learn about yourself from what happened? What is the message from the interaction?

I had a staff person who, during a meeting, was really blunt and harsh towards another person. After the meeting, I asked her to think about what had happened. Why had the interaction solicited such a strong response from her? She had not realized her response was so blunt and clearly emotionally charged. I was able to help her see something, just by providing some feedback right after the situation occurred.

For some, using creative ways to reflect will be more helpful. For example, you may find it useful to use a journal to record your experiences and feelings. Looking back and reading your own entries may give you insight into your state of mind. If you have been writing about someone at work, take a look at what you are writing about her or him. Read your words carefully to see what is factual, for example, actual things the person said or did, and what is part of your judgment or you projecting on to that person. If you write, "Tina is so arrogant, she thinks she runs the office," you have written a judgment. In your mind, you may have a long list of reasons why this opinion is justified; however, it is still a judgment about the other person. You can also delve more deeply into what you have written. Ask yourself: What specifically is making me uncomfortable? What is it exactly that is upsetting me? You want to start to see the possibility of a different dynamic between you and Tina. Consider how you can look at the situation in a more empowering way.

Another way to see more clearly is to create images representing how you feel about a work situation or colleague. These feelings might be expressed by drawing a picture or creating a sculpture from playdough, basically any creative way to try to translate the emotions you are feeling into something more concrete. Once you've done this exercise, take a look at what you have created. What does the image show you? What does it say about your state of mind? What do you now see about yourself?

In order to appreciate what is really happening at work, you need to be open to the possibility that your opinion, your judgment, can be changed. If you are so locked into your justification of why you hold your views, it will be impossible to allow space into the situation and there will be no room to see what is really happening and no willingness to make things different. Seeing who you really are requires an intense dose of honesty. You will need to drop deception, resistance, and self-justification. Being honest with yourself is a prerequisite to improving self-awareness. I encourage you to make the decision, right now, to be open to having a different view, to see people in a different light, and to work with this potentially uncomfortable journey of seeing your own blind spots.

Reflection Exercise

The questions below will help you think about where your blind spots might be. Spend a moment considering each one.

Am I afraid to change?

_____

Do I need reassurance? Do I need to be acknowledged?

_____

Do I treat my co-workers with respect?

_____

Do I blame others? Do I blame others frequently?

Am I afraid of failure?

Am I worried about what people will think?

Am I patient?

Do I appreciate others' contributions?

Do I need things to be perfect?

Do I need to be in control?

Do I listen?

Do I need to be right?

Do I take responsibility for my actions?

Do I like who I am?

Do I complain easily? Do I complain frequently?

Do I appreciate constructive criticism?

Do I need people to like me?

_____

Can I stay calm?

_____

Am I always honest?

_____

Do I value people equally?

_____

Do I talk too much?

_____

Am I critical?

_____

Am I polite? Do I say please and thank you?

_____

Do I procrastinate?

_____

Do I appreciate myself?

_____

Review your answers above. Circle the three questions that you would like to reflect on.

Understand Yourself

You have some information or direction about your blind spots, how you come across, and how you do things—now what? How can you readily understand this information in order to make it useful to your career and your life? Reflection is a powerful tool to raise your awareness. It allows for introspection and an opportunity to learn more about your fundamental nature. It helps you become more self-aware. When we reflect, we should let our minds sit with the situation or feedback that we have received. Usually, our minds are in many different places and love to jet around between past, present, future, fantasy, and reality at the speed of light. So even clearing your mind for a moment to think about the feedback you have gathered is an accomplishment.

In order to reflect on new information, you need to give yourself the space to do so. This might mean physically, for example, by giving yourself quiet time to think about a situation or reflect on what happened. Removing yourself from a situation or a person may be what is needed to gain the physical space you require. Having time away from a situation or person allows for clearer insight to arise. Space may also take the form of time; that is, you might need to allow time to pass in order for your subconscious to work away at what is going on. Time allows the emotional elements to become more defused, so that there is greater clarity about what happened.

A great tool to use for reflection is a technique established by Toyota[3], and often used in the manufacturing industry to find and remove waste, errors, and defects. It is called the Five Whys. By repeatedly asking the question "Why?" (five is a good rule of thumb), you can peel away the layers of symptoms, which can lead to the root cause of a problem. In our context of self-reflection, we also can ask *why*? Why am I like that? Why did I react that way? Why do I always do that? For whatever answer comes up, you can ask "So what?" or "Why?" again. If you can be truly honest with yourself, you will start to see deeper connections between your blind spots and who you are.

Let's go back to the example I described earlier involving my colleague the ogre. After seeing him with his family, I was able to see my blind spot about him. I could see more clearly that I had an issue with this particular person and that I treated him, overtly or covertly, poorly. So my next step was to reflect. Here is the conversation that emerged using the Five Whys questioning:

Me: Why does he bother you so much?
My mind: He's loud and overbearing.
Me: Why does that bother you?
My mind: I can't stand people like that.

Me:	Why can't you stand people like that?
My mind:	They're not disciplined.
Me:	Why do you care if they aren't disciplined?
My mind:	If you don't have discipline you're not productive.
Me:	Why do you care if they aren't productive?
My mind:	If you're not productive, you aren't valuable to society.

I have, quite harshly, judged him as not being valuable to society. Whether this is true or not no longer matters. This conversation points me in the direction of my deep-seated values and beliefs. These values and beliefs are influencing me to think and act in a certain way. There is nothing wrong with having deep-seated values and beliefs, but the exercise of reflection will allow you to more clearly identify what yours are. Then it is up to you to decide whether they are valid or fair to apply to a given situation or to a person. In my example, I started to realize that I value being a productive member of society. While there is nothing wrong with having this value, I can take a look at whether I am applying it in a fair way in this and other situations. I could go deeper to try to understand why I hold this value so rigidly.

One of our most pervasive patterns is to justify ourselves. Our mind will leap to justify our reactions, words, opinions, and judgments. The book *Leadership and Self Deception* uses an entertaining and highly instructive story to show how self-deception undermines personal and organizational performance. In the story, the main character slowly starts to see how he is betraying himself in almost all aspects of his life. Once he becomes aware of this and starts to take responsibility for change, both his work performance and family life greatly improve.[4] How do you betray yourself? Have you ever convinced yourself that a lie was worth telling? Have you ever justified your anger towards someone? Have you ever made a mistake, but not owned up to it? Have you ever discounted what everyone else was saying because you were so attached to your view? Justifying our thoughts and actions is something we all do. Perhaps protecting ourselves is innate and primal. No one likes to feel vulnerable. When you reflect on your own situation, be mindful of how much you are convincing yourself that you are right and why. When you listen to all the storylines and conversations going on in your mind, take a look at how much is related to making yourself feel justified for your actions or non-actions. Examining your thoughts in a more critical and honest way will help you reflect on what is really happening around you.

Over a period of time, you may begin to identify a pattern of thinking sooner, and more easily. The process of reflection allows you to start distinguishing your perception of what is happening from what is actually going on. Going through the reflective process helped me understand that I place a great deal of value on discipline and productivity. If I think someone does not hold these same values, it is very easy for me to be critical of him or her. I started to see how frequently my view on situations was tainted by this critical projection. By separating the bare facts from your projection, you will see situations more clearly and the instant emotions that are created start to wane and have less power over you.

Reflection Exercise
Review the three questions you chose in the previous reflection exercise. Why did these questions resonate with you? Try the "Five Whys" Exercise.

(i) *www.inspireyourcareer.com*

Act in a Different Way
The hardest part of dealing with your blind spots is having the willingness to change. Once you see and reflect, are you willing or able to act differently? In that moment at the park when I saw my colleague as another human being, I realized that I had a choice. My mind could seduce me to ignore what I see and tell me he is still an ogre and that my resentment is justified. I could hold on tight to my perception, or, I could let it go. I could let go of my judgment, let go of my resentment, let go of my frustration—just let it all go. If I choose the former, and continue with my usual pattern, I will get the same result. I will continue to feel frustrated, ir-

ritated, and resentful. I will fill each working day with these emotions and the associated stress. If I choose the latter, if I make a conscious choice to act differently, and let go of my judgment, a new possibility emerges. If I can see my colleague as he was with his family, as another human being, there is an opening for a different outcome. I might start to feel calmer around him, less agitated, less frustrated. My workday will not be as stressful. Even though he has not changed, I have decided to change my reaction to him. In his book *True North*, Bill George says that "When you can...be open to new ways of doing things, the change you can accomplish is almost unlimited. The discovery journey never ends."

One of the magical things that often happens when you are able to change your pattern of behaviour with another person is that the person responds to that change. If you are able to provide more space within a situation, others tend to respond to having that extra space. Their habitual reaction to you may also shift. You can create a genuine opportunity for a habitual pattern of behaviour between you and another person to stop and for a new pattern to emerge. By being willing to act on the knowledge gained by seeing and reflecting on your blind spots, you can dramatically change your relationships with others. The result is a more positive, empowering environment that will bring out the best in both parties.

Reflection Exercise

Based on your response to the reflection exercise above, what opportunities do you have to change your behaviour?

_____

_____

_____

Acting on your blind spots means choosing not to follow your usual patterns; it means seeing the alternatives and making a decision to do things differently. The process of seeing, reflecting, and acting on your blind spots is not for the faint of heart. You must have courage, resolve, and patience with yourself. It is a journey, with lots of opportunity to learn along the way. Deep-seated beliefs, values, and projections can take a long time to really see in an objective, clear manner. Even if you see them, it can take a long time to detach them from your thoughts, words, and actions. Breaking cycles of behaviour is not easy. You need to open yourself up and be willing to be vulnerable. This is not a place that most people want to go.

Committing yourself to a journey of greater self-awareness is the first huge step. It acknowledges that you are not perfect, that there is room for improvement, and that you *want* to be a better person. Having this desire will help you to open up to actually seeing what is happening in your interactions at work and beyond. By reflecting and acting on your insight, you will tap into your own source of greater confidence, happiness, and wisdom.

Inspire Your Career Tips

- Ask your boss, colleagues, friends, and family for insight into behaviours that annoy or frustrate them.
- Once a day, reflect on actions or words that didn't quite turn out right. Why didn't they work? How can you do things differently in the future?
- Practice letting go of judgment and fear.

CHAPTER 4
Workplace Success

"And will you succeed? Yes indeed, yes indeed! Ninety-eight and three-quarters percent guaranteed!"
Dr. Seuss

Everyone wants to be successful; being successful gives you a sense of accomplishment and satisfaction. It feels good to do your job right and do it well. You feel successful when you are able to make a difference through your workplace, for example, with clients, customers, or other staff. Workplace success can influence the level of reward and recognition you receive from your boss, your colleagues, and your organization. Being successful is your ticket to getting noticed by higher-ups, being promoted, and earning more money. In this chapter, we'll discuss the many ways to pave your path to a successful career.

Show Initiative

I was once sitting beside the president of a large, national sales company, who appeared to be in his early forties. I asked him how he had gotten to where he was, given the fact that he was so young. He said when he first started with the company, he volunteered for anything and everything. In one instance, he volunteered to set up a presentation for his boss. He finished the set-up and his boss invited him to stay and listen to the presentation. He ended up meeting all kinds of people that he would never have met otherwise and listened in on a highly strategic discussion to which he never would have normally been privy. Showing initiative at work is a great way to get noticed, especially if it is done in a collaborative way. Jump in, and do not be afraid to offer your assistance. Having a "can do" attitude attracts positive energy.

What are practical ways to show initiative? If your organization has any committees or taskforces, consider joining one. Most organizations have permanent or ad hoc committees: there might be a social committee or a health and safety committee that you could join. Find out who chairs the committee and get more information about becoming involved.

Another way to show initiative is to bring forward a potential project to your boss or team. This might be based on making an improvement to a process or trying out something new and innovative. Take the time to consider how to approach your boss with your idea, who needs to be involved, if there are any costs, how long it might take to complete the project, etc. Often we see problems in our workplace. It is very easy to articulate what is wrong, however showing initiative in this case means thinking of possible solutions to the problem. Pause to consider the issue more carefully, look at it from different perspectives, and speak to others who are affected by the same issue. You may be able to solve your own problem. If you can't solve it and need to bring it to your boss, think about why you see it as a problem, whom it affects, and what the possible alternatives are to resolving it.

You can show initiative by asking questions, being curious about what is going on, and being inquisitive about how to do things. You may notice a colleague or someone in another department doing something that you do not know how to do. Ask questions to find out more about what they are doing and how they are doing it. Self-motivation is also helpful and includes taking the time to research things you do not know or understand, reading relevant books and articles, and educating yourself as much as possible about your job, your organization, your competitors, and your sector. Taking initiative means staying open to opportunities that arise; for example, if, in a meeting, a note- or minute-taker is required or there's a request for someone to do some research on a topic, do not be afraid to raise your hand and offer to help. Usually in any kind of team meeting, tasks may come up from the discussion, which need to be completed by someone on the team. Even if you have never done the particular task before, you can get help and it will be a wonderful learning opportunity. It is also a good idea to let your boss know that you are open to learning new things and working on new projects. This gives your boss the heads up that you are willing to learn.

Keep in mind that there is always a balance between taking initiative and being seen as a good team player. You do not want to alienate others because they feel you are overly ingratiating yourself with your boss. Stay balanced in this regard by keeping others informed and involved in what you are doing, so that they too are participating in the experience. You can ask someone else to take a lead in a project or ask others to participate with you. Sharing any new knowledge that you have acquired with colleagues will help you balance being a team player with your own advancement. You can also use humour to lighten up a situation. Showing initiative in order to learn new skills and improve yourself will demonstrate itself to your colleagues very differently than if you show initiative in order to show up someone else or to nurture your ego. By being active and engaged in your work, without alienating colleagues, you will increase your visibility, which will support you in being provided more growth opportunities.

Be Organized

I remember asking one of my staff for a document she had worked on and it took her two days to track it down. To enhance your ability to perform your role in as stress-free an environment as possible, think about all the ways that you can be organized. You want to be able to locate information quickly and easily. An excellent system for organizing documents and email will help cut back on wasting time looking for things and will help with your time management. Document organization may, depending on your environment, mean both hard and soft copy management. Think through an intuitive way to organize your folders (hard and soft) so that documents are easy to retrieve and save. A great person to speak to about this is an experienced administrative assistant. Usually they have a lot of knowledge in this area and can give you some insight on how they organize their files and what might work for you.

Email management

Email management is a key area, particularly given the volume of email that most people receive. Ensure that you are knowledgeable about all the tools and applications available in your email system.

Find a framework for naming folders and saving emails. Consider flagging emails coming from your boss so that they have a higher priority in your inbox. Another key to email management is the "look at it once" practice. Precious time is wasted when we reread emails that we are not ready to deal with. Setting time aside each day to deal with your inbox is a good idea. It is also useful to periodically look at where your emails are coming from. Sort your deleted folder or inbox by sender. Are emails appropriately coming to you? There may be opportunities to remove yourself from certain internal distribution lists, to unsubscribe to newsletters, or to redirect mail to a more appropriate person. The delete key is also a very valuable resource. Holding on to hundreds of emails is usually completely unwarranted and only adds to the feeling of burden and stress. Regularly delete emails from your various folders. If you have not looked at it in the last six months, you probably do not need it.

Time management

In order to improve your time management skills, you need to know where you are spending your time. If much of your time is spent with clients, then your time management should revolve around how to maximize the time you have with your clients, while finding time to do your required administrative duties. If your time is linked to your boss's schedule, then you need to find a work rhythm with your boss that fits around when your boss gives you assignments and is available to answer your questions or review your work. Try to understand the other person's pattern and style and use that knowledge to its maximum potential. For example, if your boss does sales calls on Mondays, you know she or he is not available to you that day. Plan accordingly. If you have available time because you are waiting for your boss, ask for multiple projects so that you are able to work on something else instead of waiting.

A major element of good time management is avoiding procrastination. A favourite saying I use for people who get easily overwhelmed is: "Just do one thing." You get things done by just starting on one thing, and then moving to the next. We can spend a lot of time thinking about a task, looking at it on our desk, wishing it would go away, or leaving it to the very last minute. All this does is waste time and make us feel anxious. Start one step at a time and cross things off your "to do" list. A "to do" list is a great time management tool. Write down what you need to do and identify your priorities. Another great tool for time management is to block off time for certain activities in your calendar. You can block off meeting-free time or block off time to get through emails or to complete a particular project. By putting a task in your calendar it becomes more concrete, and has a greater chance of getting done.

Manage multiple demands

As we all know, technology continues to have a profound impact on our work environment. The most significant change is the speed with which information can be obtained and exchanged, which, in turn, has accelerated the demand to act on the information and to continue its movement through our systems. At any moment, you will have multiple demands, tasks, and projects that need your attention. The skill associated with managing these multiple demands is an art, not a science: you require both experience and good old common sense. One tool is to write a daily list of three things to do. If anything does not get done, it can be rolled over to the next day.

You should get into the habit of asking about the timeline of every single file, project, or task that you are given. Always ask the person giving it to you when they expect it back. At that moment, if you feel the date is not achievable, negotiate on the spot with the person. In addition, if at any time you are having trouble managing your workload, you need to speak to your boss to get direction. Ideally, you have created a running list of the tasks that you have. You should record the date that you received them, the date that you started them, how long they should take, and when you expect to complete them. When you go to your boss, sort the list according to what you think is the priority. This will help you and your boss assess what your workload is so that priorities can be shifted and timelines adjusted. Do not forget to keep your boss and others informed of your progress on tasks and projects.

When you are assessing the priority of your various demands, consider which have the most affect on others, with the first priority being your clients. For example, if one of your tasks has a direct impact on client service, it should score high on the priority ranking. Projects or tasks that are more internally focused tend to be those that can wait. You should also consider if, within the list, anything could be taken off completely. This can happen because of changes with your clients or external factors. Can any tasks be combined or completed at the same time? For example, can you do administrative work between meetings? You can also assess whether the task can be reduced. For example, instead of a detailed, full report, can you do a briefing memo and have the backup research available? You can also think about whether the task would be better completed by another person or a small group. The need to prioritize tasks is constant and is further complicated as you try to manage personal responsibilities. Appreciate that managing multiple demands is part of the environment where we work and live. Do your best and do not hesitate to ask for help.

Balance your day or week

Often people think about work-life balance as a big picture—an overall assessment of one's ability to balance work and personal time. I have always found it useful to think about balance in the short term. That is, can you balance your life today or over the course of the week? This approach ensures that you do not allow stress to climb unabated over a long period of time. Instead, you can reduce your stress on a more regular basis so that it does not build up and become unmanageable. For example, you might make it a point to take a coffee break with colleagues or go for a short walk or run an errand at lunch. I work out at lunch three days a week. I started doing this at the very beginning of my career and have vigilantly stuck with it for close to twenty years. I know that this has significantly reduced my stress level and optimized my ability to think clearly and remain calm. Your stress-relievers might be different; a chat at the water cooler, a call to a loved one, watching a funny video, going shopping at lunch or stretching for ten minutes. Working within the parameters of your job, it is important to balance your day or week in order to manage your stress level. Remember, this is not someone else's job or something that someone else is going to do for you. It is your job to take care of your mind and body. Think about what your needs are and be flexible in trying to incorporate strategies that will help you stay balanced.

Build On Your Strengths

Often people have strengths that can be further developed in order to achieve greater success and job satisfaction. I wish that early in my career someone had helped me to identify that leading people was one of my strengths. This insight would have moved me along my career path faster and helped me better understand where to focus and what to leverage. It took many years for me to understand what my strengths were and how to build on them.

How do you identify your strengths? You may have some insight from your boss from a performance review or from informal feedback. You may get insight from others who you are in contact with. Ask your family members or your friends what they think you are good at and what they think your strengths are. Even if the feedback is not directly work-related, you will get some insight. You should then consider what you feel your strengths are. One way to think about this is to identify when you feel the most confident in your job. Marcus Buckingham, in his book *Go Put Your Strengths to Work*, talks about freeing your strengths and spending a week focusing on the activities that truly make you feel strong and empowered. Think about what tasks or activities make you feel happy and fulfilled when you are doing them. Everyone will be different, but you might notice that you love to organize people or events, or you can't wait to analyze sales data, or you love to write, or you feel confident speaking in front of large groups. Together with the input you received from others, this should give you a good start on knowing what your strengths are.

Once you have a sense of what these strengths are, you can look for opportunities to build on them. This means that you can look for opportunities to use your strengths and to more consciously put them to use. For example, let's say you receive feedback that you are good at selling. You could try to be included in a sales discussion or negotiation with a larger client. You could seek out someone more seasoned, who you feel is strong in sales, and observe how she does things. You could ask to meet with the star sales person in your organization in order to gain more insight into how to improve your own selling skills. Knowing your strengths can also help you identify training and development opportunities for yourself. Knowing that you are good in sales may help you articulate that you would like more training on ancillary skills such as public speaking, time management, or whatever the case may be. Other opportunities you can seek out include participating in a special project, or volunteering to take on an initiative. These will give you a chance to use your strengths in a different environment.

Reflection Exercise

Fill in the blanks.

At work, I succeed most when I

_____

_____

I feel the most confident when I

_____

_____

I enjoy doing tasks that are

_____

_____

The tasks I dislike at work are

_____

_____

How can I use my strengths at work?

_____

_____

Stand in your Clients' Shoes

No matter where you are in the organization, you have clients to whom you are accountable. If you are a teacher, your clients are your students and their parents. If you work in the finance department, your clients are both internal (the people whose salaries you pay) and external (the vendors you pay). If you are working in a call centre, your clients are the people you are speaking to. Who are your internal and external clients? As you will learn, clients are a powerful force. If you do not live up to their expectations, they can easily become disenchanted. Then there is a risk of either losing them or dealing with ongoing conflict. One of the best ways to approach client service is to always put yourself in your clients' shoes. Try to see the problem or issue from their perspective. Try to acknowledge the challenges and difficulties that your clients face. Every organization's success has some dependence on positive client relations. If we lose sight of things like client needs, client preferences, or client expectations, we can negatively affect our competitiveness or, at minimum, client satisfaction levels.

Being client focused means treating clients with respect, having patience, and taking responsibility for your role. Try to maintain a perspective that has a larger scope than your own personal view, so that you see the client as a component of your success and the success of your organization. This is not easy, especially when you are tired or stressed. Imagine trying to listen to a client complaint at the end of a particularly stressful day or trying to resolve an issue when a client is yelling at you. Try to remember it is not about you—it is about them. Do your best to remain calm and collected. Clients are a great source of information about what is and is not going well. It is easy to see how organizations flounder when decisions are made by people who are further and further out of touch with the client. The client is really important to the success of the organization and you are an important connection to the client. Your interactions with your clients and their staff are very important. Even though you may be dealing with a junior person from your client's organization, every interaction contributes to creating a reputation and brand for your organization. It can be difficult to see this in your day-to-day role, but working with clients and being client focused is an essential component to making your organization work. You are contributing to the image and reputation of the organization you work for. Always remember that the work you do is really important to both your clients and your organization.

Have a Positive Attitude

As we discussed earlier, attitude is part of your professional image. The attitude that you carry with you, that you choose each day, is a strong indicator of what you can expect back. Negative energy is difficult to work with and, unfortunately, easily transferred from person to person. Think about a day when you came to work in a bad mood. How many people did you negatively affect? Was that necessary or desirable? Alternatively, think about what happens when you are positive and energetic. People are drawn toward this. Attitude is something you choose and something you have control over. I once had lunch with someone who was very successful. He was well respected, smart, healthy, had a lovely family, and a great job. He should have been exceedingly happy. When I asked him how he was doing, he said, "Same old, same old, life can be such a drag." This comment had nothing to do with the reality of his situation and everything to do with his attitude toward his life. Imagine the amount of energy and effort it takes to maintain this negative attitude. Imagine all the people who suffer because of it: his wife, his children, his co-workers, and his boss.

Having a positive attitude is something that you can work on. You can actually practice shifting your perspective and seeing things differently. Be aware of your mood, look at how you are feeling, and recognize how you influence others. Even if you are in a bad mood, for whatever reason, you can still smile at people, stay courteous, and say "Good morning." You would not appreciate someone projecting their anger or frustration toward you. The opposite is also true. We are in control of our words, our tone, and our actions. Find the small ways that help shift your mood and use them consciously to help you stay positive. For example, perhaps looking at some pictures of family or friends makes you feel better, or going outside for some air, or playing your favourite music. Taking ten deep breaths is also a great way to realign your body and mind and give yourself a fresh start. Project a more positive attitude at work and see how well your co-workers receive it.

Reflection Exercise

Generally, am I positive or negative at work?

How can I demonstrate a more positive attitude?

_____

_____

_____

Work Hard

This is definitely something my mom taught me; she is the hardest working person I know. With a Grade six education she managed to raise six kids virtually on her own. Now close to 70 years old, she still works full time in addition to babysitting her grandchildren three days a week. In her view, hard work is not drudgery, it is a source of pride and joy.

Working hard with the right kind of attitude means we tackle work as if it is a pleasure to do so. We have a sense of gratefulness that we are able to work and that the income allows us to have a certain lifestyle. Working hard means doing things well, and doing things right, from the start. It includes respecting the small tasks, which also need to get done in order to keep things running smoothly. If you have something to do, take the time to plan it at the beginning, so that you have the best possibility of success. "Measure twice, cut once" as the saying goes. Treat your work with care and be committed to doing it well. Working hard seems a little out of favour these days with the focus on work-life balance, but the two are not mutually exclusive. Working hard does not mean that you have no other life or you work crazy hours. It means that when you are at work, you give it your best effort. Employers quickly see this attribute in people and it becomes a way to get noticed and become more successful.

Demonstrate Respect

Respect really is a universal attribute; it supersedes everything. Everyone should be treated with dignity and respect and the only way that it is possible is if you fundamentally believe that everyone is worthy of respect. This includes the co-worker who has her head in the sand, the colleague who never knows when to be quiet, the peer who warms up exotic smelling food every day, and the noisy person in the cubicle beside you—everybody. Most of us think of ourselves as being respectful, but sometimes there is a disconnection between this belief and our actions. We often have deeply imbedded prejudices or low tolerance of certain things. You can learn a lot by observing your thoughts and behaviours towards others.

Ask yourself if you've ever participated in office gossip, criticized someone in front of others, or had a loud, heated argument with a co-worker. You can ask yourself why this occurred and what was really at the heart of the issue. You can also explore negative feelings toward another person. Why do you feel a certain way? This is important because your body will follow your mind; that is, if your mind is made up that someone is incompetent, your body, through your words and actions, will follow this belief. You will be more inclined to treat the person as if they were incompetent in your day-to-day interactions. Another way that the principle of respect can be lost is when the culture of an organization allows behaviours like yelling, swearing, or denigrating others to occur unchecked. This is totally inappropriate, but once it is imbedded in the culture, people lose themselves, and start to behave in the pattern that has been established. Do not succumb to this. If your co-workers are engaged in vicious or gratuitous gossip, you have a choice. You can:

- participate actively by contributing to the discussion;
- participate passively by listening to the discussion without objecting;
- walk away from the discussion; or
- say something to the group to raise their awareness about their behaviour, such as "Wow, you guys are all over X. I'd feel pretty horrible if you were talking about me like that." Or "I wonder how you would feel if someone were talking about you that way."

A colleague who was recently promoted to a manager position was appalled when she first started working in her department. Staff members openly gossiped and criticized others. This behaviour had been allowed and now it had a firm hold on the team. Her first weeks were focused on helping the team see and stop the behaviour.

A workplace that lacks dignity and respect can create negative and poisonous energy, which affects everyone. Always treat people the same way you would want to be treated, regardless of what is going on around you. Being respectful is a quality that is highly admired and that helps set a standard for the environment around you.

Be a Good Listener

Most of us think we are listening, but the person speaking would probably beg to differ. Have you ever, while listening to someone, answered your phone? Looked at your emails? Interrupted the person while they were speaking? Lost track of what the person said? Not made eye contact? Then you've been there, not really listening. This is a skill that we can all improve on and that makes a huge difference in how others perceive us. If we can learn to really listen to what others are saying, we get much more in return. Listening is a basic form of respect. If you listen, you are saying that you care about that person and that you are interested in what they have to say. If you are not listening, you are saying the exact opposite; you do not really care about them and you are not interested in what they have to say.

I have a terrible habit of cutting people off when they are speaking. I feel like I know where they are going with the conversation so I cut in and try to finish things up. Whenever I remember, I make a conscious effort to pay attention and stop myself from cutting in. Active listening takes practice and awareness, so you can catch and correct yourself if you are not listening. Experiment with this in your next conversation with someone. Commit to yourself that you will not interrupt or allow your mind to wander during the conversation. See what happens and how the conversation feels. Being a better listener means you will hear things that you might otherwise have missed. You are more aware of the non-verbal communication that is going on, including body language and subtle undertones. Being a good listener also helps you to be more conscious when you speak. Listening is a valuable skill that can positively affect your relationship with colleagues and clients alike.

(i) *www.inspireyourcareer.com*

Giving Feedback to a Colleague

We'll devote a whole chapter to dealing with conflict, but the advice that I'll give now relates specifically to a situation where a colleague's behaviour is affecting you and others. While there are clearly many different approaches to this, using honey over vinegar generally works best. If you are addressing a concern with a colleague, try to be direct, objective, and clear while showing concern for the other person. As an example, imagine that there is a woman in the office who loves to complain. She is oblivious to how much she complains, although many other people feel the ripple effect of her constant whining. You decide to say something. You could, in front of everyone, say, "Sara, you are the biggest complainer on the planet—it's ridiculous!" How do you think Sara would feel? The words are cutting, and have a lot of emotional power behind them. While Sara may take the comment to heart and reduce her complaining, there is a higher risk that she will dismiss your complaint or get her defences up. Sara may be no more enlightened about her behaviour than she was before you spoke to her. So now all you have is a really hurt or angry Sara.

Let's try a different approach. You say, in private, "Sara, you are a great member of our team. I have some feedback for you that I think will make you even better. I do not know if you've noticed this, but you often complain to others, which leaves them feeling negative about the great work the team is doing. Would you consider trying to complain less?" This approach is direct, objective, clear, and shows concern for Sara. While she may not like what you've said, your words are going to resonate. This approach will have the greatest chance of enlightening Sara about her behaviour by helping her to notice when she does complain. If you're going to address an issue, remember to separate the hard facts from your emotions or projections on what happened. The facts will keep the conversation grounded, particularly if it is difficult. A tough message can always be delivered with honesty, integrity, and an intention to be of benefit to the other person.

You receive an offensive email from a colleague. You:
a) Let the colleague's boss know.
b) Do nothing.
c) Let your boss know.
d) Speak to the person to let her know why you feel the email was inappropriate.

Appreciate Diversity

Appreciating diversity means truly respecting every distinct element of diversity within your organization: diversity of culture, diversity of language, diversity of experience, diversity of opinion, age diversity, gender diversity, and geographic diversity. We can learn to see the wisdom, skills, and value in the unique opinions that each person brings.

If you are fairly young, think about how you treat an older colleague at work. Maybe you find him irritating or irrelevant because he's not adept at change, he does not know how to use technology, and he is just not with it! Well, let's, for a moment, look at the bigger picture. What does he bring to the table? Since he has been with the organization for a long time, he knows his way around and knows how to get things pushed through the system. He would be an excellent ally for a project that you want to implement. He could give you advice on who to speak to or how to proceed. He might give you access to his network to help your project along. Appreciating the diversity that he brings to the organization can help you. And if that is not enough, try to imagine that one day you too will be his age, and you may be just as irritating and irrelevant to others in the organization. How will it feel?

Situations where cultural or religious diversity are demonstrated at work can be triggers for discomfort and hostility. Be aware of your own biases and lack of knowledge and understanding of other cultures. What would your reaction be if someone were praying in the hallway at work? What if a co-worker wears a sari to work every day? What if your colleague says he can't join you for lunch because he is fasting? Particularly in these situations, take the time to educate yourself about the traditions and beliefs of others. Think of your reaction when someone has a thick accent and is clearly from another country. The person's communication may be more challenging to listen to. Are you able to remain patient? It is important to be respectful of the diversity in your workplace and stay open-minded in all your interactions with others at work.

Inspire Your Career Tips

- Find opportunities to take initiative.
- Establish good management systems for your files, emails, and your time.
- Discover your strengths and leverage them.
- Always treat everyone with dignity and respect.
- Address a concern with a colleague in a direct, objective, and clear way while still showing concern.
- Do things well, right from the start and take pride in your work.
- Appreciate all kinds of diversity.

CHAPTER 5
Building Your Skills

"Leadership and learning are indispensable to each other."
John F. Kennedy

In a broad context, skills are abilities that we acquire so we can complete job functions involving people, things, or ideas. Building your skills is your responsibility. While it is easy to look to an employer to take responsibility for your development, ultimately you are the one who has your best interests at heart and who is able to assess which skills you need. The hardest part of starting your career is that you do not know what you do not know. It is even difficult to articulate what particular skills you are looking for. Have an "It's all good" attitude towards skill development, especially early in your career. You can learn new things from different people, from different situations, and from proactively seeking learning opportunities. If you build skills early and quickly in your career, you will be able to reap the rewards sooner in your life. Identify and seek out any opportunity to improve yourself.

There are certain skills that become the foundation for your future success. In this chapter we are going to focus on the five skills that I consider the most important to move up in your career and to get noticed and promoted in your workplace. There are a number of skills and behaviours that employers look for in employees, such as flexibility, integrity, and organizational, and analytical skills. However, the focus of this chapter is on skills that will carry you right through to becoming the leader of an organization. Here are my recommendations for five top skills, which you can start developing now:

- Execution
- Communication
- Self-awareness
- Being a team player
- Critical thinking

In addition, we will talk about the incredible benefits of building your skills through volunteer participation on a board of directors or other non-work related committees.

Execution

I am defining execution skills as the ability to complete a task well, on time, and within the resources provided. This is the "doing" skill that applies to how you actually complete your job responsibilities. Execution has elements of both hard skills and soft skills. Hard skills relate to industry, profession, or job-specific processes, procedures, tools or techniques required to complete a task, like writing software, applying tax law, or operating a machine. Soft skills relate to behaviours and people skills like being empathetic, positive, or ethical. Let's analyze execution skills using a simple example so that you can apply it to your own job and try to identify the hard and soft skill components of execution.

You are a customer service representative. What are the hard skills you need in order to successfully execute your job? You may come up with a list that includes:

- Answer the phone efficiently and effectively
- When necessary, transfer callers to the appropriate person
- Do not keep callers on hold too long
- Do not disconnect callers
- Do not let the phone ring too long

What are the soft skills that are required in order to execute your job well? You may come up with these additional points:

- Be respectful and friendly to callers
- Be patient with callers
- Be as helpful as possible in connecting the caller to the right person
- Demonstrate empathy towards callers

As the example illustrates, both the hard and soft skills are important in execution. The soft skills will usually determine the degree to which people involved in the execution were happy with the outcome. Keeping with the customer service representative example, part of your job will be letting callers know that their complaint can't be resolved. Although this is part of your hard skill execution, the outcome can still be satisfactory to the caller, depending on how well you execute on the soft skill side. You may be excellent at responding to complaints from a technical perspective, but if you ignore the softer aspects, such as being empathetic while communicating, you will not be viewed as successfully in your ability to execute.

Try to identify what hard and soft skills are required to execute your day-to-day responsibilities well. Execution skills require that you are organized, manage your time well, see what steps need to be taken, and are able to plan. You need to think through any resources necessary and communicate along the way to make sure you are on track. People who are excellent executors do not procrastinate; they execute in a systematic way. If they identify barriers, like lack of resources or not enough time, they think creatively to come up with what is possible. When you think of execution, picture yourself as the superhero of getting things done. You are fearless and undaunted by the task ahead and you use your execution superpower to tackle it head on.

Reflection Exercise

What hard skills are required in my job?

_____

_____

_____

What soft skills are required in my job?

_____

_____

_____

Which skills listed above do I need to improve on?

_____

_____

_____

What can you do to improve your execution skills? Ensure that you:

- Understand what hard and soft skills are required to be successful in executing your role.
- Understand exactly what you are supposed to be doing. If you are not clear, keep asking questions.
- Consider what resources you require and find a way to get them.
- Identify an approach to get projects done, along with a timeline.
- Break down large or complex projects into manageable tasks, each with their own timeline for completion.
- Set clear, realistic expectations with everyone whose assistance you require about what you need and when you need it from them.
- Communicate with others, as required.
- Check in with your boss to make sure you are on track.
- Get feedback after you complete a project to understand how things went and to learn about possible areas for improvement.

One last point regarding execution is to welcome the incidental learning that can occur as you perform your role or work through a new assignment. For example, as part of a project you are given, you have the opportunity to organize a meeting. While this might sound mundane, it is an opportunity to learn how to book a room and equipment, how to set and distribute an agenda, how to facilitate a meeting, and perhaps develop a presentation. These are all excellent execution skills that you are acquiring. Remember to seek feedback on how you did on these tasks so that you can improve next time.

Communication
Written
"Practice makes perfect" is a great adage to apply to improving your communication, whether written or oral. I was shocked when I

first started working to learn that I could not write. "How can this be?" I thought. "All those years of university and I can't write a memorandum?" Well, apparently not. I needed to work on everything: grammatical structure, using appropriate punctuation, being clear and concise, and focusing on the information that the recipient needed. Generally, we learn to write essays in school, which are lengthy. I had taken it for granted that all the writing I had done in school prepared me for writing well in a work setting. This was not the case. In contrast to the lengthy papers I wrote in school, writing in a work setting needs to be crisp and focused. Learning to be clear and concise in your communication is much harder than you might think.

If you are asked to write something, such as a memorandum, presentation, or report, give yourself enough lead time so you can be sure you are doing the basics, like spelling and grammar checks. Reread your own work to make sure that it sounds right. Be careful to avoid slang, short forms, and other habits that you may have become accustomed to with everyday electronic messaging. Ask yourself if you have clearly described, as applicable, the issue, the background information, any analysis that was done, and recommendations or conclusions. Have you answered the original question? Does the communication meet the objectives that were set out at the start? Have you considered what the recipient of your written communication will think? Usually when you are junior in an organization, you may be asked to prepare a first draft of a presentation or document, while someone else finishes it and takes it to the next step. Ask the person you wrote the draft for to give you feedback, or at least to give you a copy of the final version of the letter, presentation, or report. Not only will you see how your work was changed, but you will also get insight into how the organization communicates. You can learn by reviewing presentations and communications written by your peers, your boss, or your clients. Whether they are good or bad, you will learn something from reading the work of others. Another idea is to ask a third party for feedback on what you have written. It could be a colleague or an administrative assistant; basically anyone who will be able to give you timely feedback.

You should also consider your written skills in the context of emailing at work. Your work-related emails should be professional and concise. In order to assist the recipient of the information, use a descriptive subject line so it is really clear what the email is about. The email itself should be kept simple, with appropriate spelling and grammar and a polite tone. You may want to highlight any item that requires action or follow up and be clear about when you require a response. Sometimes, something called negative confirmation may be appropriate, again, in an effort to reduce the time required by the other person to deal with your email. Negative confirmation is when the sender indicates that unless she hears back within a certain timeframe, she will assume that the receiver agrees with the content of her email.

Oral

In oral communication, be conscious of the words you use, the pitch of your voice, the speed at which you are speaking, how loud you are, and the clarity of what you are saying. In basic, straightforward dialogue with another person, make sure that you maintain eye contact. Listen to what the other person is saying. When you speak, speak clearly and honestly. Speak from the heart and speak to the heart of the matter. Speak respectfully at all times. You can also improve the impression you leave when you speak by being engaged in what you are saying. This does not necessarily mean using wild hand gestures, but you can bring your speaking to life by adding passion, interest, and feeling to it.

When you first start your career, it is unlikely you will have to speak to a group, but do take every opportunity to do so. For example, you may be able to get involved in a training session where you present a portion of the material. Or you may be able to speak about some of the slides in your boss's presentation to a client. You might have the opportunity to present something at your next team meeting. Speaking in front of a crowd is an excellent skill to build. In situations where you are speaking to a group or making a presentation, be sure that you arrive early enough to check that everything is organized and ready to go. Take a few deep breaths before you start to calm yourself down. When you are speaking, look at your audience, engage them, use their names if you know them, and ask if anyone has questions or comments. The key to speaking is to be prepared, be relaxed, be yourself, and be authentic.

Non-verbal

This type of communication happens when nothing is being said. Raise your awareness of the messages you are sending to others with the attitude that you bring to a conversation, your posture, or your facial expression. These are all important forms of non-verbal communication. Your attitude, for example, may demonstrate superiority or impatience. If this is how you feel, the person listening to you will feel that attitude and it will affect the interaction. Your posture will also say a lot to the other person. Are you slouched in your chair and not making eye contact? This sends a clear message that you are not interested in what the other person has to say, even before anything is said. An open, relaxed posture will set the tone that you are available and open to the communication. Your facial expressions will also expose your true feelings. Rolling your eyes when someone makes a comment is just as clear as yelling "As if!"

Another way that non-verbal communication becomes palpable is when it emotionally contradicts what is being said. For example, if you are angry with a colleague, no matter how carefully you choose your words, the anger will come through in non-verbal ways. The underlying emotion will surface non-verbally, through your eyes, through your facial expressions, through your body language, and through the tone of your voice. Even though your words may be unemotional, the other person will pick up on the anger from the non-verbal cues that you are emitting. Another example is picking out the person in a meeting who is bored or impatient. We could name a dozen non-verbal cues that a bored or impatient person will exhibit: looking around, pulling out a phone, rustling paper, tapping feet, or closing their eyes. A great example of when non-verbal cues are very important is in an interview. Often, the person interviewing you will judge whether you "fit" within the organization based on the overall impression that you create. It is important to pick up on all the non-verbal messages you are both receiving and giving in order to have the best chance of being hired. With awareness, you can improve upon both recognizing cues in others and understanding your own.

Also worth mentioning is the often forgotten value of silence— a wonderful non-verbal communication tool. In our fast-paced world, we seem to have lost the ability to be silent. We feel obliged to fill every second with noise or activity. Silence can be used in many ways. It is a great way to transition from one situation to another. For example, before starting a presentation or beginning a meeting, you can wait that extra 15 seconds until the room is silent. It does not have to get to the point of being uncomfortable, but it is a very subtle reminder that something fresh is starting and it helps people leave their prior activities behind. One of the best ways to deal with a difficult conversation is to pause, letting silence literally bring in some air and space to the conversation. Silence is also useful to give yourself time to think. Instead of panicking because you do not have an immediate answer, literally sit back and think. Let the silence allow your mind to use its natural intellect.

Silence is also necessary if you intend to listen to the other person. Listening is not happening when you are speaking. For some of us, it takes a lot of effort to let people completely finish what they are saying and to listen attentively, with all our senses, to what is being said, both verbally and non-verbally. Learn to value silence as a wonderful tool in improving your listening and communication skills.

Self-awareness

Have you ever watched a hamster going around and around in a hamster wheel? The hamster expends so much energy but never gets anywhere. Sometimes we are on a hamster wheel, running and running, but going nowhere. We expend a great deal of energy but the effort seems painful and futile. We do things over and over again in the same way hoping for a different result. In our workplace, there are many examples of people on the hamster wheel. Here are just a few:

- A sales associate is always on a rampage. Nothing is ever right; it is everyone else's problem that he has not met his sales target.
- An analyst constantly tells people how busy she is and how many problems she is solving.
- A lawyer routinely pulls all-nighters at work. He is quick to rationalize the behaviour; the firm demands it and his clients expect it.

- A call centre representative loves to socialize and keep up with what is happening. She is indignant when asked about her unmet volumes.
- The marketing assistant talks incessantly about a lost client. He laments over what happened, what could have happened, and what should have happened over and over again.

In each of these cases, the behaviour of the person creates an ongoing pattern, which has negative implications for that person and for others who work with her or him. You can see how easy it is for the people described above to view themselves as being right, and to have a passionate opinion of how everyone and everything else is causing their problem. Each person I have described is on the hamster wheel, going around and around with habitual patterns of behaviour. In each of the situations described, the person can choose to get off the wheel; unfortunately, they can not see that they are on it.

Have you ever felt you were spinning on the hamster wheel? Perhaps you are spinning on a wheel of aggression, self-absorption, self-doubt, criticism, or fear. Self-awareness is one way to identify that you are spinning on that hamster wheel. It is only in the moments that we realize we are on the wheel that we can choose to get off. For that moment, we can choose to let go of the aggression, self-absorption, self-doubt, criticism, or fear that is keeping us spinning. We can let go and just be who we are. Let's look at the examples again, assuming that the people see their pattern and choose to stop it.

- The sales associate realizes his aggression comes from being afraid of losing control. He stops blaming people and takes responsibility for his actions.
- The analyst sees that her insecurity is at the root of her behaviour. She becomes more conscious about her words and actions.
- The lawyer realizes he desperately needs to be needed. He starts to let this go and differentiates between real work needs and his own needs.
- The call centre representative understands that she wants to

be liked by others and craves attention. She begins to balance her work demands with her naturally outgoing personality.

- The marketing assistant sees that his behaviour is a way to deflect criticism. He is afraid of failing. He takes a kinder approach with himself and tries to be more open-minded to feedback.

Getting to this level of insight in ourselves is not easy. Becoming self-aware is an ongoing journey.

You may have glimpses at work of feeling really good, confident, and proud of what you are doing. Maybe you have a good day where things go really smoothly. In those moments you feel like you have stepped off the wheel. There you are, feeling present, happy, and fulfilled. Then someone criticizes your work or gives you an unrealistic deadline or does not give you credit where you think it is due. Your mind easily starts to spin and you resume your pattern of blame, doubt, and fear. You get back on to the wheel, and around and around you go.

Realizing when we are spinning on the wheel is easiest when there is a particular situation or observation to reflect on. For example, the day after an interaction with Alice, she approaches you and says, "I don't appreciate the way you treated me yesterday." You may have a completely different view of the interaction that occurred with Alice. Before you react, consider that the situation is an opportunity to be more self-aware. Why does Alice feel the way she does? What exactly did you say or do? Really allow yourself to think about what happened. Contemplation is best done when you are alone, in a calm quiet space. You do not necessarily have to analyze the situation. You can just contemplate it. Hold the situation or the emotions in your mind, very gently and very lightly. Just let them sit there. Let your body's natural wisdom bring forward insight.

Another method you can try is to imagine yourself literally getting into the body of the person who you affected most significantly during an interaction. Try to visualize what the person saw and heard you say. Using our example, try to connect to how Alice might have been feeling during your exchange. Take in Alice's situation, concerns, and fears. Let Alice's situation wrap around you. This will open up space and allow insight to arise. Over time, as you get better at being able to reflect, you can actually see things from a different perspective. The rigidity and tightness of a particular situation start to soften and you become more aware of other people, your impact on other people, and ways in which a situation could be handled differently. We are all on the hamster wheel at various points in our lives. By improving our ability to reflect, we will start to see the choices we make about whether we get on or off the wheel.

Be a Team Player

Being a team player means that you are able to stay open to the dynamics of a team environment, that you are able to listen and really hear what others are saying, and that you are willing to let this input inform and feed into your own thinking and contribution. Being a team player means that you always keep the greater good, that is, the interests of your organization, at the forefront of your mind. This means, for example, that within a team, if two individuals are vying for the same scarce resource, the individuals will see beyond the needs of their own project and be able to base the decision on what will achieve the greater good for the organization. The two people will work collaboratively with the other members of the team to make the best decision possible. Whoever gets the resource will be grateful and the person who does not will support the decision that was made. This is what it means to be on a successful team: working together to achieve more than you can achieve alone.

Being on a team means being able to balance being a contributor of ideas and fresh perspectives with being a listener so that you can synthesize what others are saying. A positive team dynamic requires trust and openness in order to get the best out of the group. How can you be a better team player? There is a saying that there is no "I" in "team." You can be a better team player by thinking of your teammates and the organization first. This does not mean you get taken advantage of. In some cases, putting the good of others first means urgently demanding money for your project. If, in your view, getting the money for your project is in the best interest of the organization, then lobbying strongly is the right thing to do. Another example of a team situation is when one person is not pulling their weight. Putting the interests of the team first means ensuring that everyone fully participates. Ask the person if there is anything you can do to support them in completing their portion of the work. Ask the person to bring an update of her progress to the next team meeting.

I was recently driving my four-year-old twin niece and nephew to the YMCA. I parked and opened the van door. My nephew had already gotten himself out of his car seat and was helping his sister undo her seatbelt. As soon as she was free she exclaimed, "That's teamwork!" I thought, yes, teamwork indeed. Being a team player means helping others whenever you can, saying thank you when others help you, being grateful and appreciative of your team members, and bringing a positive, helpful, and open attitude to team meetings. The best team players have a sense of humility, which allows them to celebrate success and share recognition with their team members. The best team players are also reliable and diligent. They work hard on behalf of the team and the organization. They are quick to take responsibility and slow to lay blame. Think about the greatest team players in sports, or people you have worked with who are great team players. They have similar qualities of being trustworthy, committed to quality, and highly respected. Consider how you can develop into a great team player.

Reflection Exercise

Are you a *great*, *good*, *fair*, or *poor* team player?

_____

Why?

_____

_____

What could you change to be a better team player?

_____

_____

Critical Thinking

Critical thinking is an extremely complex skill, which you will continue to develop throughout your career. There is no better time to start than right now. Webster's New Millennium Edition defines critical thinking as "the mental process of actively and skilfully conceptualizing, applying, analyzing, synthesizing, and evaluating information to reach an answer or conclusion." My simplified definition of critical thinking is to use everything you know and feel to make the best decision. Usually, when someone thinks we should have seen something coming, or known what to do, critical thinking is the skill to which they are referring. Let's take a specific example. Justin's boss is really upset at him because something important fell through the cracks. "How did you miss this?" the boss asks, exasperated. Justin was collecting information for months as part of a report he was compiling. He didn't realize that he needed to verify the information that he was collecting. While we could argue that the boss should have spelled this out for Justin, or that it was an understandable mistake, let's focus on the role of critical thinking in this situation.

The boss is upset because he feels Justin has not used critical thinking. If we look at our definition, this means that the boss felt that with everything Justin knew before he came to the job, and with what he saw and understood about the information he was collecting, Justin should have realized that it needed to be verified. Here are some examples of the clues that Justin may have received, which should have triggered his critical thinking:

- It crossed Justin's mind a few times that this task was pretty easy.
- Justin wondered who was verifying the information.
- Someone mentioned verification, but he didn't think it applied to him.
- He considered asking his boss about whether the information should be verified, but he shrugged it off.
- Where Justin worked before, they always verified the information.

Critical thinking is related to developing your judgment, to knowing what to do in a particular situation, to know what information to gather and what questions to ask. Critical thinking skills improve as you experience more situations, resolve more issues, deal with more people, and have a better understanding of systems. However, you can start building your critical thinking skills now. Below are ways to incorporate critical thinking at work:

- Clarify and analyze the meaning of words or phrases—Specific industry jargon and acronyms are common in workplace environments. When you are new to a role or an industry, you will be tempted to guess or assume what something means, without really being sure. Clarify what words and acronyms mean.
- Evaluate the credibility of sources of information—Ensure you know where information came from, particularly if you are relying on that information to complete a task. How reliable is the source?
- Question deeply—raise and pursue root or significant questions—The first answer we get from asking a question may not give us the full picture. Ask more questions to ensure that you fully understand the issue being discussed. Why? Is a great question to ask.
- Develop intellectual humility—Having an open mind at all times helps us avoid jumping to conclusions or assuming we are right.
- Listen critically—When you listen fully, you can listen for emotional content and other clues that will tell you more about what is being said than just the words.
- Examine or evaluate assumptions—It is common to do things in an organization in the same way they were done in the past. What underlying assumptions are being made about your project or task? Are the assumptions valid?
- Distinguish relevant from irrelevant facts—We are often overloaded with information. It is essential to discern between relevant and necessary information versus information that is irrelevant or unnecessary. What information is critical? What is tangential?

- Explore implications and consequences—Always think ahead to what will happen if an action is taken or a decision is made; for example, think of the people who might be affected. Ask questions such as "What happens next?" and "What if we do this?"
- Generate or assess solutions—You should always be thinking about solutions to problems that you encounter in your role. What are the possible solutions? What are the pros and cons of each possible solution?[5]

Which do you choose?

You have a feeling you are processing something incorrectly. You:

a) Do nothing; hope no one will notice.

b) Seek clarification from your boss.

c) Review the steps you've taken, consider what might be missing and what options you have.

In any situation, use all your knowledge and experience and all you know and feel about the situation to determine the best course of action. My sister was the banquet manager for a major hotel. During a large banquet for a local college, she noticed a change in the mood of the crowd. The group was young and bar sales had been brisk. The lively crowd was turning boisterous and rowdy. She was trained to deliver excellent service and be completely customer-focused; however, in that moment, she used all her past experience, her instincts, and her assessment of what was happening to make the decision to shut down the event. Using critical thinking skills, she came to the rapid conclusion that the potential risks of allowing the event to continue outweighed the need to deliver service. During your career, and increasingly as you advance in your career, you will need to make judgments in the absence of complete information and with insufficient time. Critical thinking skills become essential in the workplace in order to make the best decisions possible. The dimensions identified above are a great starting point for the kinds of things to consider as you develop your judgment and critical thinking skills.

Build Skills through Volunteering

A fantastic way to develop the skills described above is to volunteer as a member of a board of directors or on a non-work related committee or group. Unlike your workplace, a volunteer is treated equally relative to other volunteers. So when you sit around a board table, for example, each board member is equal, each person has the same right to speak, be heard, and to have an opinion. This diffused power structure means there is no higher-up to make decisions. Decisions are arrived at through a conversation, open debate, and, usually, consensus. It is an entirely different dynamic than that of the competitive, hierarchical structures in most organizations. Therefore, the environment for learning is rich.

When I was 24 years old I became a volunteer for United Way. Through this, I was connected to a children's agency that United Way had provided with seed money, but was considering retracting due to the agency's poor overall condition. I joined its board and soon after, became board president. What the board accomplished for this charity is one of my proudest achievements. Over a relatively short period of time, every aspect of the agency was improved: the number of children served, its physical buildings, parent satisfaction levels, staff satisfaction levels, its finances, the board, funder relations, etc. I was able to use and learn many skills. Even better, there is immense gratification in volunteering your time for something you believe in.

Learning from a volunteer position comes in many ways: You learn about the organization that you are volunteering for, which will open your eyes to some of the amazing work that is going on in your community; how to prepare for and communicate during a meeting; how information is gathered, debated, and consensus is achieved around issues; and you will learn what governance means and how not-for-profits work. You will learn how to stay open to others' ideas and opinions, even when they are very different from your own. You will learn about strategic planning and how the organization's vision and mission can be realized. All of these are amazing skills to bring back to your current role or to put on your résumé for a future position.

How do you get yourself onto a board or other volunteer committee? There are several ways you can do this:

- Apply for vacant positions that are posted on charity bulletin boards and other networks.
- Participate in services that help match volunteers to positions.
- Speak to people in your network and let them know you are looking for a volunteer board position.
- Choose an agency whose mission and values resonate with you; this might be due to a personal experience with a particular cause. Write to them about your interest in being a volunteer for them.
- Proactively seek information about being a board volunteer by contacting the current board chair.

www.inspireyourcareer.com

The most challenging aspect of getting on a board is that you may not have much board experience. To offset this, you need to consider what skills or experience you can offer to an agency. Perhaps you have technology, marketing, or finance skills that you can bring to the board. Spend some time thinking about how to market yourself for a board position. You might highlight the fact that you bring age diversity if, for example, the board is made up of older people and you are younger. You might bring cultural or gender diversity to a board. Another way to get noticed is by volunteering for events that the organization you are interested in sponsors. This allows you to get to know the organization, and they to get to know you. This relationship building will give the organization a chance to see that you are reliable, bright, and interested in their cause. Cultivating relationships this way can lead to a larger volunteer position in the future.

Inspire Your Career Tips

- Consider the value of silence as a communication tool.
- Make a conscious effort to raise your self-awareness.
- Demonstrate that you are a great team player by contributing positively to team activities.
- Follow through on nagging feelings, hunches, and intuition. Your critical thinking is probably at work.
- Volunteer as a board or committee member at a favourite charity to gain valuable skills.

CHAPTER 6
Finding Mentors

"Mentor: Someone whose hindsight can become your foresight"
Author Unknown

Having a mentor is a fantastic way to enrich your career. Mentors can teach you skills, share knowledge, help you see opportunities and challenges that you might not have seen on your own, and provide advice and guidance through many situations. There is something very unique about a mentoring relationship; there is a natural sense of goodwill within the relationship. In the best cases of mentoring, both parties allow themselves to be a bit vulnerable and to open up to the other person. There is a genuine intention by the mentor to be of benefit to the other person and there is a genuine openness in the protégé to receive that benefit. This exchange is extremely powerful. In this chapter, we will discuss three kinds of mentoring relationships—formal, informal, and silent—along with tips on how to get the most out of these relationships.

What is Mentoring?

The origin of the word mentor comes from Greek mythology: Mentor was a friend of Odysseus. When Odysseus left for the Trojan War he placed Mentor in charge of his palace and his son, Telemachus. On several occasions in the *Odyssey*, Athena assumes Mentor's form to give advice to Telemachus or Odysseus. While mentoring can occur in many different forms, it traditionally refers to a one-on-one relationship between a more experienced person (a mentor) and a less experienced person (a protégé), which is intended to advance the personal and professional growth of the less experienced individual.[6] Mentoring research has demonstrated the power of mentoring in relation to career success, measured both in terms of income and in hierarchical position.

In a research study involving in-depth interviews with a cross-section of almost 300 executives and leaders, respondents were asked what they felt was the most powerful method of developing leadership skills. Respondents most often selected mentoring as the most powerful method.[7] There is no doubt that mentoring works and that generally the benefits are mutual, positively influencing both the mentor and the protégé. During your career, you should seek out mentors whenever possible. There is such a huge body of knowledge available through the personal insight and life experiences of another person.

Formal Mentors

A formal mentorship is one in which the relational role, that is, of mentor and protégé has been established and agreed to by both parties. This can occur in a formalized mentoring program at your workplace, where you are assigned to someone specifically for the purpose of being mentored. This can also occur where you and another person agree to a mentoring relationship, which means that you can initiate the creation of such a relationship. If you are fortunate enough to work in an organization with a formal mentoring program—fantastic! Take full advantage of it. Related to this, it would be perfectly appropriate to ask in a job interview if the organization has any kind of mentoring program available.

If you do not have access to a formal mentoring program at work, you can seek out mentors from your circle of contacts. Before you embark on this search, consider what objectives you have in seeking out a mentor. For example, if you are interested in a particular industry and want to learn more about it, finding a mentor who is well established in that industry would be very advantageous. If you are interested in a particular position, you may want to seek out someone who currently has, or previously has had, that position. Alternatively, if you are interested in becoming an entrepreneur, seeking a mentor who is or has been a successful entrepreneur will be helpful.

In my experience there are three key elements required to succeed in a formal mentoring relationship: a good fit between the mentor and protégé, in terms of personality; clarity about the purpose and objectives of the relationship; and clear logistics and parameters outlining how the relationship will operate.

Good fit

When I first became a CEO, one of my staff organized a luncheon so I could meet one of the founders of the organization. Barbara was retired, but had been CEO of the organization at one time. I liked her instantly. The minute I got back to my office I called her and asked if she would mentor me. She agreed. We met for over a year, about once a month, over breakfast. Our time together was immensely beneficial to me. I often brought questions that only someone who knew the history of the organization could answer. I think the added bonus was that Barbara also enjoyed the meetings. She felt reconnected with the organization that she had started from scratch and that she still felt passionate about.

The first sign of a good potential mentor is that you admire the person. There is a quality or style of that particular person that resonates with you. Do not hesitate to ask if she or he would be willing to go for a coffee or lunch with you. The worst thing that can happen is that the person is too busy and says no. At least you have put the idea out there that you would love to meet to ask a few questions. When you consider your circle of contacts, think about your family members, friends' parents or siblings, people from a previous job, and people in your current workplace. You can also ask your boss or your human resources department about being matched to a mentor. The key is to not be afraid to put yourself out there. In my experience, people are honoured to be asked to mentor and, if at all possible, will try to accommodate your request.

Once a mentoring relationship has begun, you will need to use your judgment as to whether it feels as if things are working well or not. In some cases, a good personal fit will come naturally in the relationship; in others, it could take some time to develop. There is also the possibility of conflict within the relationship. Your mentor may, for example, feel strongly that you should or shouldn't do something. Your mentor may have a completely different management style than you. You are the only person who can judge whether the relationship continues to be beneficial, even though you have differences of opinion, or whether the relationship is strained and you feel it is too difficult to continue with the person. In either case, you should be open in communicating with your mentor so that no matter what the outcome, you remain on good terms with the other person.

Clarity of Purpose

Clarifying the objectives of the mentoring relationship will make the process of mentoring much easier for both parties. Take a moment to consider what exactly you want to achieve from the relationship. What do you hope to learn and what areas are you most interested in discussing? Try to write down the main objectives you have so that they can be easily communicated to your mentor.

Once you have established your objectives, it is easier to gauge how much of a commitment and how much time you are seeking from the other person. For example, the questions that you have may be able to be answered in one sitting over lunch with someone. Alternatively, you might be looking for someone to have a more consistent relationship with. You can be very clear with the person that you would like one hour of time to ask some questions about her or his career path. In these cases, you do not even have to use the term mentoring (even though that is what will be going on), you are simply asking for professional assistance from that person. If you are looking for an ongoing relationship with someone, it is fair to be clear about that up front so the potential mentor can make an informed decision about whether she or he has the time and can take on the commitment of the role.

In addition to your overall objectives, you want to be prepared for your meeting(s) by thinking through specific questions you have for the person. Depending on who they are and their experience, craft questions that you feel they can help you with. Here are a few to get you started:

- How did you get to where you are? What was your career path?
- Did you always know what you wanted to do? How did your path change over time?
- What is something you have learned that has had a large effect on your life?
- If you could go back would you change anything?
- What is your strategy for success?
- What are the ideologies that you believe in and live by?
- What is the biggest mistake you made and wish you could

take back?
- What inspires you?
- What is the best advice you ever received?
- How did you balance family and work?
- What was your biggest conflict and how did you resolve it?
- Are you still passionate? How do you stay passionate?

You may also structure meetings by topics. This means that you bring a specific topic to each of your meetings, and the topic becomes the basis for discussion. Your list of topics could include: How to be a Leader, How to Increase My Skills, or How to Show Initiative. These topics could either be planned in advance, possibly at the first meeting with your mentor, or you could bring a new topic to each meeting. Another way to identify topics is to keep a log at work of issues that arise that would be good topics for discussion with your mentor. During the period that I was meeting Barbara, I always kept a notepad handy and jotted down topics and questions that I wanted to bring to our next breakfast meeting.

Clear Logistics and Boundaries
In addition to being prepared with questions for your mentor, ensure that expectations are clear for both parties. Is this a one-time meeting or are you looking for an ongoing dialogue with the person? If ongoing, consider:

- How often will you meet?
- Where will you meet?
- When will you meet?
- Who will set up the meetings?
- How long will the relationship last?

You should also ask your mentor if there is anything she or he is hoping to learn from you. You may have a perspective or experience that would be helpful to the other person. For example, many baby boomers are struggling to work effectively with Generation Y. As a member of that generation, you may be able to provide useful information to your mentor about how to attract, recruit, and retain people like you into their organization.

Which do you choose?

You ask a mentor for advice, but hate what he tells you. You:

a) Let your mentor know how you feel.
b) Find a new mentor.
c) Say thank you and let it go.
d) Think about the advice you got. Does it hold any insight? Is there another way to look at it?

Another element to a successful mentoring relationship is to know when it should end. Do not be afraid to end the mentoring relationship once you have a sense that there is nothing left to talk about or your objectives have been met. Simply be honest with the other person. Say something like: "I really appreciate all that you've done for me and I think it's time for me to work with what we've discussed. Perhaps we could stay in touch but end our formal sessions." It would also be gracious of you to check in with your mentor periodically, once your sessions start, to make sure that the time commitment and effort still make sense for her or him. This gives your mentor an opportunity to end the relationship.

Informal Mentors

Informal mentoring occurs when you have a relationship with someone that, by its nature, lends itself to mentoring on a fairly regular basis. You haven't actually asked, "Will you be my mentor?" but in fact, the person is. The most common type of informal mentoring occurs with your boss. She is a person who you will be working most closely with, have time to speak to, ask questions of, learn from, and generally get to know better. Another example of informal mentoring can occur with a person whom you admire and see on a fairly regular basis outside of a work context; for example, a sports coach, or a relative with whom you are close.

With informal mentors, the mentoring that goes on is more transactional, that is, the routine interactions between the two of you create the transfer of knowledge and skills. As you and your boss interact, you are receiving information, knowledge, and an example of how things can be done. Likewise, if you are part of a sports team, the routine interaction with your coach will also provide guidance and advice. What is often missing in an informal mentoring relationship is the more focused opportunity to ask questions, as was discussed in the formal mentoring relationship. Consider taking or making opportunities to ask questions of your boss, coach or other informal mentor that are outside your normal roles. In the case of your boss, you will need to be careful about the kinds of questions you ask. He won't be the right person to ask about alternative career choices, for example. Notwithstanding, there will always be some benefit to learning from another person who has achieved some type of success in your opinion. Check out the questions previously listed for those that would be appropriate in the situation.

Silent Mentors

I'm a big believer in working in silent mentoring relationships. What is silent mentoring? Silent mentoring occurs when you notice a quality or style in another person and you make a conscious effort to emulate it. In most cases, the other person has no idea that you are doing this, so the exchange is "silent." The key here is to raise your consciousness when you notice something admirable about another person that you feel would be of benefit to cultivate in yourself. Instead of it simply being a passing thought— "Wow, she's so cool"—you pay closer attention to what the person says and does, as well as the person's non-verbal cues. What precisely is the quality in the person that you are admiring? Once you have identified it, you can work to bring it into your own pattern of behaviour. For example, I once met a woman who was president of a children's centre. Although I did not interact with her often, I always admired how calm and gracious she was. She had a positive impact on me and others. I made a conscious choice to develop these qualities myself. I created an intention and objective to be more calm and gracious. I then looked for opportunities, for example in a meeting, to mimic this behaviour.

This tool is meant to draw out qualities you have, but that perhaps are less dominant. The idea isn't to lose sight of who you are or to try to pretend to be someone else; you are simply trying to bring qualities that you like in others into your awareness and therefore into your behaviour. For example, you may be very driven and decisive and feel that this makes you very successful. You meet someone who is also decisive, but you notice that this person is able to laugh a lot and seems to have more fun. What opens up in your mind is the possibility that you can be driven and focused, and have fun at the same time. What previously seemed like contradictory qualities now appear possible to maintain at the same time. For silent mentoring to work, you have to believe that who you are is not cast in stone; you are malleable. You can start to see how positive qualities can be cultivated and actually incorporated into who you are.

Reflection Exercise

Describe a quality you admire in another person.

_____

_____

_____

Why do you admire it?

_____

_____

_____

How can you incorporate this quality into your own style?

_____

_____

_____

Hire or Ask for a Coach

Another way to obtain a mentor is to hire a coach or ask your employer to hire one for you. Hiring a coach may be expensive for you when you are first starting out, but depending on what you are trying to work on, a professional may be the best way to achieve your objectives. Career coaching can be an effective way to help you through a transition or help you to identify what you need to do to get your career on track. There is also the possibility of your employer paying for a coach for you. You will not know unless you ask. If you are interested in receiving coaching sessions, you can make a case to your employer about what you would specifically like to work on and demonstrate how the coaching will benefit you and the organization. Ideally, you should incorporate measurable outcomes into your request in order to strengthen support from your employer.

ⓘ www.inspireyourcareer.com

You are a Mentor Too!

You may be a mentor to someone right now, and not even know it. I remember when I was in my twenties feeling shocked when one of my younger sisters described me as a mentor to her. Perhaps I had a vision of mentors being old and wise, or that there was this invisible age line you had to cross before you could legitimately be a mentor to someone else. Everyone in some way sets an example for others. Right now, you probably have a family member, a friend, or a neighbour, who turns to you for advice or thinks of you as a role model. It is important to be a good example for others, especially to those who look up to you. Choose your words with care and always be supportive. Something you say today could plant a seed in another person's mind…a seed that takes root much later in their life. This is also true in your workplace. It won't take long before you aren't the rookie anymore, and others will look to you for guidance and assistance to support their careers. You will have ample opportunity to be a mentor to others. Simple things like encouraging new hires, taking the opportunity to expand their thinking, giving them a compliment or identifying a strength that you see in them are all wonderful ways to be a good mentor to another person. Try to remember how important mentors are to you when you step into the role of being a mentor.

Inspire Your Career Tips

- Seek out formal mentors from your network and your circle of friends and family.
- Be prepared by knowing what your objectives are and what questions you would like to ask.
- Take the opportunity to speak to informal mentors about your career.
- Look for qualities in others that you can emulate and make your own.
- Be a good mentor to others.

CHAPTER 7
Career Transitions

"It is the journey itself that makes up your life."
Homer, The Odyssey

All transitions in life have feelings of excitement and trepidation tied in with them: happiness about what you are moving to, some grief or sadness about what you are leaving behind, and sometimes a sense of uncertainty as to whether you have made the right choice. Career transitions are no different. You will face many different transitions in your career and each will hold its own unique collection of risks, possibilities, and emotions. Try to stay aware of and receptive to the process of transition and to use it as another opportunity to learn more about yourself. It is also important to keep in mind that any transition is easier if approached with a positive attitude. For example, you might commit to "bloom where you are planted." With this kind of attitude, there is no wrong answer, regardless of the transition.

Transition Between Jobs

This is probably one of the hardest things to navigate during your career. You wonder: "Is it time to leave this organization?" "I have an opportunity somewhere else, should I take it?" There are no easy answers to these questions. You really have to look deep inside yourself to try to uncover the answers that are right for you. What you can do is try to identify what is motivating you to leave, or conversely, to stay in a position. Something that is very helpful in this process is to have a career plan in mind. I meet young people all the time who say they have no idea what they want to do in the longer term; however, if you probe a bit further, you start to hear about the things that motivate them, that inspire them, and that they are really passionate about. They might say that they want to work internationally or that they would love to lead a large team, or be able to do research and write. If you have not written down your career goals, now, as you contemplate a transition, is a good time to do so. By knowing where you would ultimately like to be in your career, you will have a barometer against which you can measure the career options available to you.

Which do you choose?

You hate your new job. You:
a) Start looking for another.
b) Resign yourself to the fact that it will be miserable.
c) Think about what exactly you don't like. Is it the culture, the people, the tasks? Find ways to address the things you don't like.

You may be thinking of leaving a job because you do not feel challenged, or because you do not get along with the boss. Or perhaps the culture of your workplace is not aligned with what you want. These are all good reasons for considering a transition. And while your next job may be transformative, it may also leave you wondering why you left your previous job. In any workplace, there will be people you get along with famously and others...not so much. Be clear about your motivation for making a move, so that you are not disappointed when you arrive at your new job. It is useful to ask yourself whether the reasons you want to leave can be alleviated in your current role. For example, if you do not think you are being challenged enough, ask yourself whether you have spoken to your boss and asked for more challenging assignments. If you do not think you're learning enough, have you asked to take more courses or be considered for a new initiative? If you dislike your boss, have you tried to see the positive qualities and ensured that you have learned all you can from her?

You should also consider whether a career stepping stone is required. A particular move may not seem ideal, but it may be a strategic choice that will get you closer to your ultimate goals. For example, you may be a manager and you want to become a vice-president. The progression to get to vice-president requires you to be a director first. However, there are no director opportunities at your current company, so you purposefully seek a new company that will give you the director title. This is a stepping stone on your path to becoming a vice-president. Stepping stones may also be necessary in order to acquire a particular skill; depending on how critical that skill is for you, it may be worth taking a demotion. For example, you may take a lateral or even lower title in order to be in a much larger, well-known organization that has international offices because you feel that the experience will provide you with contacts and expose you to business in other countries, which is what you are passionate about. So even though you are possibly taking a demotion, the potential payoff is high, both in terms of bringing you closer to what you want to do as well as putting you in an environment where there are more opportunities. And like all decisions, never underestimate the power of your intuition. Listen to it when you are contemplating a transition to another job.

Transitions are also more complicated when others are affected by your decision. For example, if you have a spouse, children, or a parent you are caring for, you need to take your additional role and responsibility to others into account when making your decision. Your decision to leave or stay in a job will have to consider these important people in your life. If you have a child, the financial impact of a job transition may be much more important to you than whether the role will be challenging enough for you. As you contemplate a transition, consider the various factors involved in the decision, and try to categorize them as advantages or disadvantages. You can then look further into whether the factors are of high, medium, or low importance to you. A very good friend of mine is CEO of a hospital and has had many career transitions in her life. The way she reflects on a possible career transition is to diagnose the tensions that might emerge. For example, you may be contemplating:

- a job that pays you more, but requires a longer commute;
- moving to a small organization from a large one, or vice versa;
- a job that provides great experience, but it is not in a field you are passionate about;
- starting your own business, but need help with the financial implications;

Identifying and understanding the various elements of your choices will help you bring greater clarity to make the best decision.

ⓘ *www.inspireyourcareer.com*

Reflection Exercise

You are contemplating a career move. What are the advantages of moving to the new position?

_____

_____

_____

What are the disadvantages?

_____

_____

_____

Look at your list of advantages and disadvantages and rank each as either of high, medium, or low importance. Review the three most important factors. What direction do they pull you toward?

_____

_____

Transition into Management

One of the most important decisions to make about your career is whether you move into management. Having people report to you will increase your earning potential now and in the future. In almost all other cases, a job position to which no one reports will, at some point, hit the maximum level of remuneration for that particular role. Other than cost of living or step increases, there is very little room to earn substantial pay raises. Taking on the responsibility of managing others significantly changes your career prospects. Managing people is a skill that, when done well, is rewarded, both in terms of earning potential and promotion potential. You can more easily move to other organizations, take on larger teams or portfolios, and increase the scope of your role, all of which lead to more money and more senior position titles. For anyone interested in having greater influence, authority, and power, it is critical to acquire the skill of managing and leading others. In my own experience, being in a leadership role is a very rewarding experience.

I would like to make a special plea to women in this regard. Women are currently underrepresented in every area of power and influence in North America. Female chief executive officers are extremely rare in large corporations. Based on 2009 data[8], there were only 15 female CEOs in the U.S.'s Fortune 500 list and 27 in Canada's Financial Post 500. Women hold only 15% of the board seats of the U.S.'s top companies and only 13% of the board seats in Canada's top companies. The numbers are also low when you look at elected members of government and owners of companies. Gender equity is one of the most basic elements of diversity, yet these numbers are from North America, one of the most developed and progressive regions in the world. Having gender equality in places of power and influence will bring more balance and diversity to the world. I strongly encourage every woman to set her sights high. Be confident that you can succeed as a CEO, a board chair, the head of a political party, an entrepreneur, or an investor. The first barrier to overcome is the one in your own mind. If you can break through that one, then anything is possible.

Moving from Colleague to Manager

If you move into management through an internal promotion, you may be faced with the potentially awkward situation of having former colleagues reporting to you. This is often hard for your colleagues; of course they wish you well, but there is some pang of regret because they did not get the job or were not qualified for the job. There may also be a sense of loss among some of your colleagues. They have "lost" you to management. They know that the relationship with you will not be the same, and it won't be. Your co-workers may be grieving over losing you in this transition. It is important to appreciate the dynamics that are going on during this type of transition and try not to minimize your promotion or overly reassure people that everything will be the same. Your colleagues, some of whom may have been social friends, can still be friends, but the relationship will change. As a manager, you now have a responsibility to do what is best for the organization. What is best for the organization, as a whole, is not always best for individuals within it. Be careful that people reporting to you are not so close that you cannot remain objective in the face of a difficult decision.

The other pitfall to watch for is favouritism, especially where some of the people reporting to you were social friends. Favouritism within a team does not even have to be real, just perceived. So be cautious and mindful as you take on your new role. Be appreciative of individual success, but ensure that you are also praising the team. Make sure that you give individuals equal opportunities to do special projects or assist you. The best approach is to be yourself and communicate openly. You can relay your commitment to the team and talk about what you would like to do to make things better for them. A good strategy is to remember all the things that frustrated the team when you were a team member and plan what you can do about them now that you are a manager. It is also a good idea to talk to your boss about your transition and seek advice on how to make it as smooth as possible.

Transition to or from a Parental Leave

Some of you will be able to perfectly orchestrate when, where, and how you will take a parental leave. For others, it will be completely unplanned. In either case, the transition to or from your leave can be a time of heightened, conflicting emotions. How long you stay off work, the flexibility you have, the economic impact, all these things will come to bear on your thinking and analysis of the best choices for you. As always, trust your instincts on what is right for you. Depending on your relationship with your boss and the organization, you may consider asking for a compressed workweek, different hours, or the ability to work from home to make the transition work best for you. Be creative and consider out of the box solutions to achieve a balance between the needs of your employer and your own objectives. I have a wonderful friend who is a managing director in a global investment firm. She has a long list of "firsts," including being the first person in the firm to ever make partner while being on a flexible workweek. She works hard, but does it from 7 a.m. to 1 p.m. She has had huge success in being both a great mom and having a rewarding career. Remember that your career is long-term, potentially spanning 40 years of your life. The choices you make and the plan that works for you will take into account your partner, your children, and your needs. You want to balance all these needs in order to make the best overall decision.

Something I have observed with many women is how hard they are on themselves, both in making decisions regarding this transition and then second-guessing themselves about the decisions they have made. For example, if they make the decision to stay home, they worry about their career. If they decide to go back to work, they feel guilty about not being home. Women with families have an incredible amount to juggle. Adding the self-imposed worry of whether you made the right choice can stress you further. Be kind to yourself. If you have made the decision to stay home, try to delight in your children and have confidence that you can return to your career when you are ready. If you make the decision to return to work, do your best there and enjoy coming home to your family. Allow yourself to be where you are and feel confident that it is exactly where you should be.

Transition Back to School

After starting your career, you will become clearer about where you want to be in the future. As part of this process, you may realize that you need additional credentials or more specific education. As you contemplate a return to school, you will need to consider a number of questions, including:

- Will I go full- or part-time?
- What is the best program for me? Will completing the program further my career objectives?
- What are the financial implications?
- Do I have any support, either financial or from a flexibility perspective, from my current employer? If I do not have it currently, can it be negotiated?
- Does my family support the decision?
- How will I change or adapt my life in order to take on school responsibilities?

- What is my plan once I graduate from the program?
- What are the future financial prospects of having the new credentials or training?

As you contemplate a transition back to school, ensure that you have given sufficient consideration to all the factors that will influence your decision. In addition, seek advice from others who have returned to school or who are contemplating a similar move. A well-thought-out plan will assist in making this transition as smooth as possible.

Transition Out of a Job

Most people I know, myself included, have been restructured or otherwise let go from a company at least once in their life. This may happen to you. Do not panic. While it is not the most pleasant experience, it forces you to reassess where you are in life, what is it that you want to be doing, and how can you get there. It is an opportunity to re-evaluate your situation and take a look around, sort of like pulling over onto a scenic lookout along your road trip. This transition is a tough one because it is so emotionally charged. Most people go through a traditional grieving process, starting with shock and disbelief that they have been let go, followed by some form of anger or depression and, eventually, coming out the other end to acceptance. This is a process, so whether you like it or not, it takes time to get through it. Being aware of this will help make it more tolerable.

Other than the restructuring scenario, you should also be alert to warning signs that your organization is giving you that could lead to your termination. Examples of warning signs include a poor performance review, lack of straightforward communication from your boss, or feeling that you are over your head or extremely stressed. These signs may point to the deterioration in fit between you and the organization. They are also opportunities to self-reflect and re-evaluate your situation. Take a good look at the information you have and ask yourself if you can turn the situation around? For example, if you have received a poor performance review, do you have the energy and skills to step up and improve? If you do, you need to have a direct and honest discussion with your boss. If you do not, you may want to get advice on how to proceed to a fair and equitable departure from the organization.

Inspire Your Career Tips

- Use your career goals as a guide when trying to make decisions about staying or leaving an organization.
- Use career stepping stones to strategically position yourself for the next job.
- Get into management as soon as possible in order to maximize earning and position potential.
- If colleagues now report to you, be yourself, be open, and be objective.
- See a transition out of a job as a fresh opportunity to review your career.

CHAPTER 8
People Report to Me—Now What?

*"By three methods we may learn wisdom: first, by reflection,
which is noblest; second, by imitation, which is easiest; and third
by experience, which is the bitterest."*
Confucius

When I first had people reporting to me, I thought, "Yippee! Now I can really make things happen." What I soon found out is that there is a complex interconnectedness and interdependency among and between teams and departments, the organization, as a whole, and external stakeholders. Authority appears to have power, but this is a myth. The real power is in influencing, role modelling, and continually being a good conduit for the right connections and information exchanges to happen. As you advance, because you move further and further away from the direct frontline work that is going on, people skills become critical. You need to be able to engage and influence people to move in a certain direction, without actually doing it for them. Your most important job is to get the best out of people in order to achieve the organization's mission and vision. In this chapter, we'll highlight some of the top things you can do to get the best out of people, which in turn, helps you become a successful new manager.

What is Different?

When you make the transition into management, and have people reporting to you for the first time, you will notice several significant changes in your day-to-day activities:

- You are less involved in the direct work of your team or department.
- You spend significantly more time in meetings, and generally deal with more administrative responsibilities.

- There is a multiplicity of needs to balance.
- You are responsible for the work of a group, not just your own activities.
- You'll realize that supervising people takes a lot of time.
- You do not get instant gratification from your role.

Even though these are significant changes, the expectation, whether reasonable or not, will be that you can start immediately and adjust quickly. Most new managers feel like they have been thrown into an ocean and told to sink or swim. Be prepared for this to be a major, intense transition in your career.

Build Credibility

One of the most important things to do immediately is to build relationships and establish credibility. People will judge your level of competence, your trustworthiness, and your consistency in your new role. Building credibility through building relationships means taking the time to get to know people, speak to individuals on your team, and understand what is going on. Do not be afraid to ask lots of questions. People love to talk about themselves and their work if you give them a chance. Trustworthiness can be established by always being honest, even when what you are communicating is difficult or challenging. Being honest means being comfortable with saying "I don't know." In most cases you can follow this up with "I'll find out." Everyone appreciates a leader who can show his vulnerability or lack of knowledge. Trustworthiness also means that you do what you say you are going to do and that you walk the talk. There is nothing more irritating for people than a boss who says one thing and then does another. If you are going to hold people responsible for being on time, then you have to be on time. If you are going to demand that a certain deadline be met, you too have to respect the deadlines set for you.

I mentioned the importance of respect in a previous chapter, but it is worth revisiting here in our discussion of being a credible boss. In order to be genuinely respectful of others, you have to embrace the diversity within your team. This means having a genuine appreciation for the different perspectives that come from people from different offices, cultures, professions, ages, experience, and education levels. You have to be totally open to having your belief system, your values, and your approach challenged. This openness allows options and solutions to appear, thereby helping you to deal with the challenges and opportunities that occur on a daily basis. The diversity within your team will be a source of creativity and innovation. Demonstrating unflinching respect, no matter what the circumstances, is a powerful way to build credibility and tap into your team's potential.

Treat People Fairly

Being treated fairly is something that stirs a lot of passion in people. Perhaps we all have a strong sense of justice and equity wired into our brains. This is consistent with my own experience as CEO; most staff complaints that escalated to me were usually about people feeling they had not been treated fairly in one manner or other. Here are a few examples of situations that can be perceived as unfair, thereby soliciting a lot of strong emotion:

- One team getting or doing more than another;
- An internal hiring process where one person is chosen over another;
- Workload allocations;
- Someone is being given additional tasks without acknowledgement or remuneration;
- One person is given more opportunities than another; and
- One person has more time with you than another.

As you can see, treating people fairly is a tricky balancing act. You need to balance the needs of individuals with the needs of the team and with the needs of the organization. You need to motivate people, but not deflate others in the process. You want to encourage and challenge your star performers, while at the same time support and acknowledge others on your team. You want to be firm, fair, and flexible.

There is no magic answer for how to manage this. You need to be aware of the dynamics within your group, ensure you are implementing fair processes, and generally trust your instinct on whether something is going in the right direction. Another tool is to use your staff as a sounding board by bringing proposed processes or new ideas to them to discuss and provide input. This will not only provide you with feedback, but also get their buy-in ahead of time. If something is really challenging, get advice from your boss, a peer, or the personnel department.

Be Responsive and Reliable

Being responsive is an important element of success when people report to you. When a person's boss is not responsive, it becomes a huge source of frustration and one of the common complaints that surface in engagement surveys or through performance reviews. When you are not responsive to another person, you are basically saying the person is not worthy of your time or your attention. You can make all the excuses in the world, that you are busy or that you have another deadline, but the bottom line is the other person does not feel important to you. When a person does not feel respected, it hurts, especially if this is coming from his boss. Being responsive means acknowledging people's phone calls, emails, and requests as quickly as possible. Even if you cannot get to the actual issue, you can still acknowledge that you received or have heard the information and you can communicate what the next step will be or when you will be able to act. Another way to be responsive in cases where the question or concern is not really your responsibility is to forward it to the appropriate person as soon as possible and let the inquiring person know you have done this, for example, by copying them on the email that you are forwarding to the appropriate person.

The follow through of responsiveness is reliability. I once had a manager who was highly responsive. She would respond to emails immediately, virtually at any time of the day or night. Unfortunately, the follow-through was inconsistent at best. So while her responsiveness was outstanding, her reliability was not. This is a deadly combination because people will start to resent the quick responses. If they feel that nothing is ever going to be done about their issue or concern, the quick response acknowledging them will wear thin. In fact, they would probably prefer no response at all, that way they do not have the expectation of follow-through. When you respond but do not follow-up, your credibility goes downhill fast. Reliability means that you are faithful to your own word and that you follow through on any commitment or promise that you make. Nothing will erode trust faster than not doing what you say you are going to do.

Reflection Exercise

Indicate true, false, or sometimes for each question:

I respond to my emails and telephone messages quickly.

I respond to requests for information in a timely way.

I complete projects on time.

I do not procrastinate.

I do what I say I am going to do.

Review your answers, what areas of responsiveness and reliability can you improve on?

Remove Barriers

When I first started as a CEO, during one of the introductory meetings with the various teams, someone asked me, "What does a CEO do?" I loved this question and I am sure a lot of people were wondering the same thing. I answered, "My job is to remove barriers, so that you can do your job." And while the answer may sound simple, removing barriers that get in the way of optimal job satisfaction, optimal effectiveness, optimal efficiency, and optimal results can be incredibly difficult. As you try to remove barriers for people, you discover that there is a web of connections between your team, your clients, other departments, existing procedures, and written policies. Let's say you want to eliminate the necessity to complete an administrative form. Your team thinks this is a great idea and you proceed. You soon find out that the accounting department relied on that form to get certain information for the financial statements; you also find out that the receptionist was responsible for filing the form and knew nothing about it being eliminated and, finally, someone points out that the form is referenced in one of the company policies, so if you eliminate it you need to update the policy. Depending on the size of your organization, trying to remove barriers will often elicit a lot of frustration.

The key to removing barriers and more generally to get things done in organizations, is to build good relationships, which we have discussed, and to have an understanding of system thinking. System thinking means that you can rise up, above your particular job or area, high enough to see all the people and things that interconnect within the organization. From your perch, you see how human resources and finance, because of their support role to the organization, are almost always affected by decisions that are made elsewhere. You see that your clients are making all kinds of demands for services, products, warranties, or pricing. You see that your technology system is about to burst. This is the perspective from which you want to remove barriers, implement change, and lead your team. By considering the larger system in which you operate, it will be easier for you to determine who needs to know, who you need input from, and whose buy-in you need. Your success in removing barriers will depend on the network you have established and your ability to quickly align the various system pieces.

Learn the Numbers

Whether you like it or not, you will have to have a basic understanding of numbers in order to be successful in your role. You may be responsible for a budget, for authorizing payroll or expense reports. Perhaps you receive monthly or quarterly financial statements that you are to analyze. There may be questions that are asked of you regarding variances, overages, etc. You need to understand what is going on financially with the department or area that you are responsible for, and ideally, you should have some understanding of how this fits into the larger financial picture of the organization. Numbers can be very intimidating, particularly if they are not an area of strength or interest for you. You need to learn. Consider where you can go for help. Do you know an accountant who could give you a tutorial on how to understand financial statements? Is there someone in the company's finance department whom you could seek help from? In my experience, the finance department in most organizations is under used as a resource for learning. This is the engine that knows the most about getting things paid, what accounts to charge to, how variances occurred, and so on. Make friends with members of your finance department: They can be important allies.

Provide Thoughtful Feedback

Providing feedback about a person's performance is a valuable, critical exchange that allows you to guide and support your staff. Feedback should be provided as close as possible to the circumstances or situation that triggered the need for feedback. This is true for constructive feedback, positive reinforcement, or praise and encouragement. Someone I know once spent hours on a project for his boss. After handing it in, he did not get any feedback. He began to get worried and consumed with the idea that his boss did not like his work. This generated fear of getting fired. At his performance review, almost a full year later, his boss mentioned the project in passing and said he had done a really good job. Keeping feedback close to the work or situation can be important in ways you may not even consider.

If someone performs a task and you do not feel that it was done well, provide specific, concrete feedback to the person. Ideally, you should provide the feedback while remaining supportive. For example:

> "Alice, I notice that there are several assumptions in this report related to the sales team. Did you verify this information? If not, I can show you how to verify it."
> "Tom, I don't feel enough effort was put into this presentation. I had asked for specific data to be included and it

was not. Let's review how this can be improved."

"Cindy, I think your creativity really came out in our team discussion today. However, I find that your follow-through is not reliable. Let's talk about how to improve this."

Try to approach each exchange with honesty and openness. Even if not everything is positive in what you have to say, the person can still feel that they were treated fairly and respectfully.

Which do you choose?

A team member is overwhelmed most of the time and is not coping with her responsibilities. You:
a) Fire her immediately.
b) Do nothing and hope she quits.
c) Solicit feedback from the person's clients, and peers and gather your own thoughts (a 360-degree review). Discuss what she needs to improve, how this will be measured, and when you expect to see results

Annual performance reviews are a more structured opportunity to provide feedback. If your organization does not do reviews, do them anyway: they are that important. Ideally when putting together a review you should be able to gather feedback from colleagues or clients that the staff member works most closely with and incorporate this feedback into your own observations. Before the actual meeting, you should check in with your own state of mind. How are you feeling about this person? Do you intend to be helpful? Again, this is regardless of what exactly you have to say. Before your staff member comes in, take a moment to reflect on your intention; for example, you might say, "I want to communicate in the best way I can" or "I will be thoughtful and balanced with my words." The next thing is to welcome them and thank them for coming to the review. You can take a few minutes to explain the process, what you have done to gather the information that will be discussed, how you will be presenting it, and that you welcome a dialogue and questions. When you are actually going over the information, provide both positive feedback and the areas of development that you would like the person to work on. With the latter, try to be as specific as possible so that the person is really clear about what you want done. One way to think of this is to imagine that you are acting as a mirror to the other person. Reflect back to them the behaviours, speech, and actions that you want them to consider. Remember, a mirror doesn't judge; it only reflects back what it sees. You are offering an opportunity for growth and development; offer it freely and openly.

(i) *www.inspireyourcareer.com*

Make Decisions

Self-help author Brian Tracy said "Almost any decision is better than no decision at all." This really holds true; there is nothing that frustrates staff members more than waiting for a decision. It paralyses their work, reduces their efficiency, has a negative impact on your credibility, and stifles innovation. Making decisions in a timely way is a critical skill that you need to develop and become confident in. When you have a decision to make, ensure you have the available facts. This does not mean you have all the facts. If all the facts were available, the person who needs the decision could have probably made it on their own. The difficulty is that, usually, something is missing and there is an unknown element to the problem. So you need to develop your confidence in knowing when you have enough information to make the decision, when you need more information, or when the decision is not yours to make.

If you have enough information, or no further information is available and it is a relatively minor decision, just make the decision and move on. Avoid second-guessing yourself or rethinking the decision afterwards. Just let it go. If it is a significant decision under the same circumstances, you can either ask for assistance or you can mull it over. The key here is to communicate with the person waiting for the decision where you are in your thinking and what you're planning to do. Say "I am going to reflect on this and I will have an answer for you in the morning" or "I want to discuss this with my boss, but I will get back to you as soon as I speak to her."

If you need more information to make a decision, be clear about what information you want; for example, particular data, statistics, or someone's opinion. Then you need to ensure the steps are in place to gather the information by a certain day or time. Again, you need to communicate that status to the people who are waiting for this decision. "I have asked accounting to do a spreadsheet of last month's returns. As soon as I have that, I will get back to you." Being clear and honest about where things are goes a considerable way with team members and has the added benefit of giving them insight into what they missed or what they could have thought about. It is a learning opportunity for them.

You may need to determine whether a decision is yours to make, or if it is yours to make alone. Given the incredible interconnectedness of organizations, it is highly likely that a decision will affect others. Do you need others in the room to make this decision? Do you need to collaborate with another department head? Do you need to defer the decision to your boss or someone higher up as the risks or consequences are more than you feel you can approve? And finally, consider if your staff can make the decision. You need to be the judge of when this is appropriate, but allowing staff to make decisions provides a sense of empowerment. This makes their role more fulfilling and enhances their willingness to take responsibility for their actions.

Embrace Ideas

Ideas are at the heart of innovation. Be appreciative of the person who speaks up and brings an idea forward. Even if the idea is not going to be acted on, it can still be recognized. In this case, be clear with the person about what the limitations or challenges are with the idea. This will validate the effort but will also provide a lesson to the person about why the idea won't work. One of the most demoralizing situations for a staff member, which is not quickly forgotten, is to have an idea shot down by his boss. How ideas come forward will vary from organization to organization, but your role as a new manager is to be open to new ways of doing things and new approaches to issues. One of the best ways to reinforce your commitment to this is to implement new ideas. Any time someone comes to you with an idea that you feel can be executed, just go ahead and do it. You still need to think through issues with the process, but if you can demonstrate that ideas get implemented, you send a clear message that empowers staff to challenge the status quo. The message tells them that they can feel comfortable and excited about bringing forward ideas and that you are willing to take risks. Recognize and reward people willing to bring forward ideas, even in a small way, to help send a strong message that new ideas are welcome and encouraged.

Appreciate and Say Thank You

People love to receive appreciation for their work. It is such a simple thing to do but as we all can attest from our own experience, we just do not do it or receive it enough. A verbal or written thank you to someone for doing a good job, or going the extra mile is powerful. When we appreciate others, we contribute to the creation of a healthier, more positive workplace. When we hold on to that appreciation, fearing that by giving it away it will take away from us, we add to the negativity in a workplace. Be appreciative to your staff as much as possible. Beyond personal thanks, public appreciation is also great, particularly if you have recognition mechanisms within your organization, like posting acknowledgements on your intranet or corporate newsletter. If this is not available to you, you can provide public acknowledgement at a team meeting. While you may not want to single anyone out, it does send a clear message to your team when someone is thanked publicly for what she has done. One of my staff made it a habit to read letters of appreciation received from clients at her team meetings. It was a positive and upbeat way to start her team meetings and gave a great boost to the individuals who were recognized. Further to verbal and written acknowledgement, small tokens of appreciation like gift cards or a small gourmet treat are always great ways to recognize people. Using a personal touch in your appreciation of staff will go a long way in building trust and commitment from your team.

Inspire Your Career Tips
- Focus on bringing out the best in people.
- Do what you say you are going to do.
- Communicate and connect when giving feedback.
- Make decisions so that things keep moving.
- Welcome ideas and input.
- Always say thank you.

CHAPTER 9
Cultivating Confidence

"I was always looking outside myself for strength and confidence but it comes from within. It is there all the time."
Anna Freud

One of the toughest obstacles for anyone, but particularly for a new manager, is feeling confident in what you are doing. Usually, new people in this role feel completely overwhelmed. Their duties are thrust upon them and they instantly become responsible for people, processes, and accomplishing a myriad of tasks. There is a multiplicity of priorities and issues that require attention, right from day one. And perhaps the hardest thing of all is that you don't know what you don't know. This chapter discusses how to feel more confident in your role, with a particular focus on new managers.

Gather Feedback

I highly recommend, as one of the very first things you do, job shadowing every person who reports to you. Even if you have moved up internally and understand the job of the people who report to you, job shadowing helps you understand how each person is performing her role. It provides valuable insight. If job shadowing is not physically possible, at least take the time to meet people individually so you can introduce yourself and get to know each person a bit better. This is the time to ask a lot questions, and suspend your desire to jump to solutions. Listen to each person and ask things like:

- "How are things going?"
- "Could you show me how you do things?"
- "Are you having any challenges?"
- "Do you have any ideas for improvement?"
- "What is one thing you really like about your job?"

- "What is one thing you wish you could change?"
- "What do you think I should focus on in the next few weeks (or months)?"

The perspectives that you gain will start to give you a clear picture of what is going on with your new team and you will quickly start to develop a list of items that need to be addressed and things you would like to accomplish. You will also start to get a glimpse of who your performers are and who may need some assistance.

Gathering feedback from your clients and other stakeholders is also important. This will be different from one workplace to another, but you can determine whether there are any client satisfaction surveys that you can review or you can consider how to speak directly to the clients you serve about their experience. What went well for them and how can the organization improve? You may have an important stakeholder, like a regulatory body that you need to develop a relationship with. Find out who you need to know in your new role and call them up. Introduce yourself and ask the person to meet with you. This is how relationships get started; you just meet and get to know each other. You also need to spend time with your boss on a regular basis, particularly when you first start, to ensure that you are progressing appropriately and continue to be on the right track. Your boss's feedback along the way will help to guide you and determine priorities.

Look for Small Wins

Looking for small wins is an excellent way to build your confidence when you first start. You have a chance to demonstrate your leadership and do something positive for your team. Perhaps, after you have gathered feedback and information, you see that there is a process that can be improved very easily, thereby saving people a lot of time and energy. By implementing the change, you have shown your ability to execute and you have made people's jobs easier. Other small wins might be in the form of low cost purchases that make a big difference to your team. I once bought a microwave for a staff kitchen because people were complaining they could not heat up their lunches. You would have thought by their reaction that they had just won a lottery. That microwave was greatly appreciated. Consider purchasing computer devices that help with ergonomic issues, painting the area where your team sits, buying some art, getting the carpets cleaned—anything that is a quick fix with big payoff from your team.

Small wins also exist in the communication area. Especially at the beginning of your role, try to communicate as much as possible and look for opportunities for people to feel well informed and connected. For example, you may find out that your team does not have a current directory of who is on the team with extensions and locations. This is easy to implement and hugely enhances the sense of order within a workplace. Your team may not have easy access to common forms or policies; simply request them or make them easy to access. Perhaps your office is nowhere near where your team is. Try to relocate or find a way to show your presence to your team on a regular basis. Finding the small wins early in your appointment to management sends a positive message about your priorities and your appreciation for your team.

Be in the Know

Sir Francis Bacon said, "Knowledge is power." On an ongoing basis, try to collect and read as much data and information as possible about your department, company, and sector. This includes things like annual reports, financial statements, minutes of leadership meetings, the website, the intranet, policies and procedures, external reports, and research. Having a sense of what is going on both at a local and more global level will give you great insight into why decisions are being made and allows you to contribute more intelligently when you have an opportunity to do so. Other ways to be in the know include attending open board meetings or annual public meetings. These could be for your organization or for your sector. You can look for opportunities to attend external conferences or professional development events. Not only will you learn something about the topics being presented, but you will also have a chance to meet other people and build your network. Finally, try not to miss out on any information that is distributed internally. This might be corporate communications, such as newsletters or announcements, or information that you get from your peers, your staff, or your boss. Knowing what is going on in the organization really helps you to feel more secure and confident in your role.

Once you gain new knowledge, try not to hoard it. Your staff will also benefit from being in the know about what is going on both internally and externally. By sharing information you elevate and empower your entire team. Find ways to regularly communicate and inform staff about what is going on within and outside the organization.

Own and Learn from Mistakes

You are going to make mistakes. We all do. If we didn't make mistakes, the learning would not be as intense and vivid. Don't get too caught up in the fact that a mistake was made. Focus instead on two very important behaviours required after you make a mistake. The first, which is critical for your credibility, is to take responsibility for what went wrong. As a manager, blaming other people or circumstances for your mistakes is deadly. You will alienate people and create a lot of unnecessary negativity and stress. Further, people who are affected by the mistake will much prefer to hear "I am so sorry, here's where I went wrong. We'll get it fixed up right away," instead of "Oh, that was not my fault, it was the marketing manager." This means that you need to acknowledge any fear and be willing to be vulnerable in front of your staff, your boss, or your whole organization. It is extremely powerful to be accountable for your actions and decisions.

The second important behaviour to demonstrate after making a mistake is to learn from it. This sounds easier than it actually is. When people make mistakes, they get caught up immediately in fixing them. If you make a big mistake about your team's schedule, you quickly try to fix it. If you process a payment incorrectly, you take steps to correct the payment. There is nothing wrong with trying to address mistakes or resolving problems, but there is virtually no learning in it unless we understand why it happened and we are clear about whether it was an isolated error or related to a more systemic problem. In order to do this, you have to really look at the mistake from where it started so that you can see what factors influenced it. Let's take each of our examples. In the first one, to correct it, you fixed the team schedule. This sounds fine, but ask yourself where the mistake started. Did you receive incorrect information from staff? Did information get to you too late? Are the forms that you build the schedule from illegible? What is the root cause of the mistake? Is it isolated or systemic? If it is isolated, you can learn from it and move on. If it is systemic, the problem is larger and requires more analysis of how to address the underlying root cause. In the second example, we process a payment incorrectly. Again, ask yourself what is the root cause. Do you lack training in the process? Was the payment unusual and if so why? Spend the time to really understand the nature of what went wrong, in order to more fully grasp the lesson that can be learned from having made the mistake in the first place. Do the same analysis when mistakes are made by your team. This will help ensure you deal with the system issues and do not make the same mistake twice.

Embrace the Competency of Others

It may seem odd to include embracing others' competencies as a way of cultivating your confidence, but there is a paradoxical reaction to having and appreciating competent people on your team. Often people fear the competency of someone who reports to them. In their mind, if that person is too good, it will make them look bad. In fact, the opposite is true. Having competent people makes you look brilliant. Your team is smart, capable, and, hopefully, the whole thing could run without you. I have always looked at team building as having the ultimate goal of the team eventually not needing you. You want to put together a team of the brightest and the best people you can find. If you let your ego or fear get in the way of recognizing others' brilliance, you diminish both theirs and yours; you start to build walls that should not be there. Find and cultivate the most competent people possible, and compliment and praise them for what they are able to do.

Which do you choose?

You have a really smart person on your team. You:
a) Cut him down whenever you can.
b) Make a point of telling him all the great things you've done.
c) Encourage him, appreciate him, and try to give him challenging work.

Trust Your Instincts

It is difficult when you are starting your career to trust your instincts. You may feel that you just do not know enough or do not have enough experience to make the decision that is before you. But you will find, time and time again, that your instincts are an excellent guide for what you should or should not do. They tune you in to the nuances of a situation and are able to provide you with valuable information. In his book *Blink: The Power of Thinking Without Thinking*, Malcolm Gladwell examines what he calls rapid cognition, the kind of thinking that happens in a blink of an eye. He refers to common situations; for example, you meet someone for the first time, or walk into a house you are thinking of buying, or read the first few sentences of a book, and your mind takes about two seconds to jump to a series of conclusions. Gladwell argues that these instant conclusions that we reach are really powerful and very important.

An instinct can come in isolation; for example, you have a feeling you should do something or not do something. You can also have a feeling based on the culmination of data, interviews, research, or planning around an issue. In these cases, your instinct is being paired with the accumulated knowledge. Trusting your instinct requires you to tune into it. You need to be aware of, and open to, a nagging pull to do something. Your instinct may feel like an aversion to going in a certain direction or making a certain choice. It may also come in the form of unexplainable synchronicities or alignment around a particular person, place, or thing. The idea is to listen to and practice trusting your natural instincts.

Understand Your Values

Do you know what your values are? We do not usually think about our values. Perhaps this is because they are difficult to articulate without a context. Most people's values will come out in full force when they are challenged. When they are challenged, your values have a way of suddenly standing up and saying, "Wait a minute—that is not right!" I once worked for someone who had very different values than I did. His line of where something remained ethical was in a different place from mine. We would often argue bitterly about whether a business decision was acceptable or not. It was only in hindsight, after leaving the job, that I felt the burden of our tension regarding values lifted. Your values will inform the choices and decisions you make and are a foundation for the behaviours you demonstrate on a daily basis.

What are your values? What is important to you? Your values will often come into play while at work. Would you accept unethical practices in your organization? Would you sacrifice religious beliefs to adhere to a work protocol? Would you betray a friendship in order to advance your career? Seeing your values in play during situations at work will help you understand what is important to you or the relative importance of one value over another. Another way to think about values is in terms of "brand." This term is used to describe the distinguishing features of a product, organization, or person. Consider what your "brand" is. What are the distinguishing features of your personality and character? Your values and your brand tend to become stronger and clearer to you as you become more confident in yourself. For example, as a new manager, you may be willing to do things that go against your better judgment or sense of values because in that role, you do not feel the confidence and power to make a different choice. Over time, confidence grows and you become better at standing up for your values in any situation.

Reflection Exercise

If you were to create your own "Golden Rule," that is, a strong principle that you always live by, what would it be?

_____

_____

List three additional values that you live by. For example, having meaningful relationships, a sense of humour or honesty.

_____

_____

_____

(i) www.inspireyourcareer.com

Be Authentic

Being authentic in your role cultivates confidence *in yourself.* We have all made the mistake of trying to cultivate confidence by seeking it externally, for example, by taking credit where it was not due to us, or overstating what we accomplished or clamouring for attention from people we are trying to impress. As the quote at the beginning of this chapter states, confidence comes from within, and is always available to us. Being authentic helps you find your confidence. When you are authentic, you are true to yourself, with no deception or excuses. This means not losing yourself; do not lose yourself in the group culture, in trying to be who you think your boss wants, or in trying to be who you think your team wants you to be. You should be the same person, seamlessly, whether you are interacting with your whole team, individuals on the team, your boss, your colleagues, or your clients. People should have the same view of who you are because you treat everyone equally. I once had a colleague who everyone complained about. She had various personalities depending on who she was speaking to. She was sweet as pie when she was interacting with our boss. She was overly friendly with some people, and a witch to others. It was amazing. The lack of authenticity in her behaviour was obvious to many of us who worked with her. Strive to remain grounded in your values, which will help you stay true to yourself.

Being authentic also means being true to others, which includes no lying, no backstabbing, and no jockeying for position. In this sense, being authentic is about honesty and respect for others. We can work on being genuine with ourselves and the people we work with. We can do this by treating others as we would want to be treated. In particular, as a leader, integrity is essential. You need to do the right thing, every time, no matter what. You are now an example to others. Your situation is different than it was before, you are being watched more closely and there is a higher expectation for how you behave and conduct yourself. One of the greatest disappointments for people working in an organization is when the leaders do not speak and act in the same way that the organization portrays itself externally or communicates internally. Have a sense of courage and confidence (not arrogance) as you take the driver's seat in your role as an authentic leader.

Inspire Your Career Tips

- Get to know each person on your team and find out what's happening.
- Act on suggestions from your team that are easy and quick to implement.
- Learn to listen and trust your instincts.
- Stay current on what is happening in your organization and your sector.
- Determine if a mistake is isolated or systemic.
- Believe in yourself and your ability to do your job.

CHAPTER 10
Accountability, Empowerment, and Delegation

"Really great people make you feel that you, too, can become great."
Mark Twain

Once you start supervising staff, the importance of accountability, empowerment, and delegation become more evident. These are elements that are applicable to each individual member of your team, but are also relevant for the team as a whole. You will have to find where you are comfortable with each staff member, in the ebb and flow between delegation and supervision, between freedom and accountability and between direction and empowerment. This is an art, not a science, and requires insightful observation on your part and a lot of communication so that there is mutual understanding at all times.

Create a Vision

Similar to the benefits of having a written career plan, it is important to develop a vision of what you would like to accomplish in your role. You may have some initial ideas based on the description of your role and your research on the company; however, it is only when you are in your role and have a chance to speak to internal and external stakeholders that you start to get a really good idea of what needs to be done. Creating a vision for your department or team will help you articulate what you want to accomplish. This in turn allows you to create a plan for achieving the objectives. In the next chapter we will talk further about involving your team in creating goals together. You, as the leader, will need to give some thought to the areas that you feel need improvement or specific goals that you would like to accomplish in your role.

I have a tradition that I started years ago. Within the first few months of starting a new job, I write out a long list of the things that need to be done. This "To Do" list is written on large poster size paper in bright markers. Then I tape it up right over my desk. When things get done they get a big fat check mark. The list is primarily for me, as a very visual way of keeping all the things I need to do at the front of my mind and to keep me focused on a day-to-day basis. The unexpected benefit has been that the list is there for anyone to see and read. I have had people in my office who read through the entire list. It is very helpful for others to understand what you are working on and what you are trying to accomplish. Your team members need to be engaged in working toward a common vision.

Articulate Roles and Responsibilities

You need to be clear about what is expected of your staff and your staff members want to be clear on what is expected of them. If you do not have job descriptions for each individual on your team, work with the individuals and your personnel department to create them. Review the job descriptions you do have and get input from the people they relate to. Creating and updating job descriptions may not sound like the most thrilling task, but it is incredibly helpful in clarifying roles. You will also be glad you did it if you have any performance issues to address within your team. In most organizations, job descriptions are woefully out of date. As you go through the process of creating or revising job descriptions, you can consider a number of issues, such as whether all duties are encompassed within each individual job description, and whether, collectively, they capture the roles and responsibilities of your team. You can check whether there is hand off from one job description to another. For example, if you have a service representative on your team as well as a team lead for that group, does the job of the service representative stop at an appropriate point and is it then picked up in the description of the role of the team leader?

Ask your team members if they feel there are new tasks that have been inherited by them that they do not feel belong to them. In small organizations, for example, staff picks up all kinds of roles like dealing with complaints, updating the website, or covering for people when they are away. It's not that it's a bad thing to offer to help, but people generally want clarity as to whether something is officially part of their job or not. Occasionally covering for someone is different from assuming you will always cover for that person. Without clarity, people get resentful of unacknowledged tasks that they are performing. The creation and revision of all job descriptions provides the additional benefit of further familiarizing your with your team and the activities of its members. Going forward, your role will entail continually clarifying who is doing what. Job descriptions become redundant quickly because of the pace of change within organizations. On a regular basis, new tasks and projects will come up that need to be delegated and managed. Staff may have special requests you are trying to accommodate and you also need to keep tabs how your team connects to other teams in the organization.

Set Performance Expectations

The job descriptions and role clarity will focus you on the activities of your staff and your team. However, it is also important to connect the activities to results. If your team does not know or is not clear about what it needs to achieve, there is little hope of achieving it. Is there a revenue target you need to meet? Are there quality indicators that you are trying to improve? Do you want to increase client satisfaction levels? Are you trying to increase revenue or gross profit? Are you trying to increase the number of clients served? No matter what industry or sector you are in, no matter if it is for profit, public sector, or not-for-profit, performance indicators are the way to focus your efforts. A maxim that is often used is "What gets measured gets done." Work with your boss to ensure that you are clear on what the performance expectations are for you and your team. If this is difficult to obtain, create your own. You should know enough about the organization, its strategic objectives, and the role of your team to be able to define a few key performance indicators. Involving your team members in this process is best. Ask, "What is the measure of our success?" and "How do we know if what we are doing makes a difference?"

Once expectations are defined, you need to hold everyone accountable. I've always found it interesting that accountability has a rather negative connotation while empowerment has a very positive one. Accountability and empowerment are two sides of the same coin; they cannot be separated. If you are accountable to deliver on something, you have to have the power to do so. Likewise, if you are empowered to do something, you have to be accountable for actually doing it. Holding people accountable means working closely with them to ensure they understand what they need to do, that how they are doing it makes sense, and that they are working at an acceptable pace. Empowerment means allowing people to make decisions as much as possible and giving them the leeway to implement their decisions. A huge mistake that new managers make is separating these two concepts. If you hold a person accountable for something that she does not have the power or authority to execute, that person is going to fail. And before they fail, they will feel out of control and anxious. Let's look at an example:

Robert is asked by his boss to deal with a complaint by a customer. The customer is upset about a product she purchased. Robert puts an order in for a replacement product and lets the customer know that she will receive a new product. The customer is happy and Robert lets his boss know what he has done. His boss is furious, "Why did you replace the product? That will cost a fortune." How do you think Robert will feel? He was asked to deal with the complaint, thus he was *accountable* for the completion of that task. However, after trying to be accountable and complete his task, his boss was upset. Robert was not *empowered* to complete the task. Accountability without empowerment is very dangerous. As you can see from the situation above, Robert is left feeling confused and anxious and his boss is also upset. The dangerous part is that Robert will always question what he is actually empowered to do. He will hesitate when asked to complete a task because he is not certain what he can and cannot do. The reverse can also be true when a manager provides a lot of leeway, but then does not hold the person accountable. In this case you end up with a person who has a lot of freedom to do nothing. In the same example, Robert is asked to deal with the complaint, but he knows his boss never follows through. He leaves the complaint on his pile of things to do. The woman who filed the complaint becomes increasingly upset and files a complaint with someone higher up. Balancing accountability and empowerment for your team members will create enthusiasm, reduce stress, and improve morale as your team works to achieve clear goals.

Reflection Exercise

Based on your role right now, what do your clients care about the most?

_____

_____

_____

Based on your answer to the question above, what results can you try to achieve for your clients?

_____

_____

_____

Follow Up and Provide Feedback

In order to give your staff the best chance of success, you need to review results with them, check in periodically, and provide feedback along the way. A common frustration is that people only hear from their boss when something is wrong. People want you to care about them, be interested in what they are doing, and in how they are progressing. In addition, regularly checking in ensures that there are no surprises, that the person, and thus the team, is on schedule, on track financially and is meeting expectations. What feedback do people need on an ongoing basis? For any given task or project, they want to know:

- Are they taking the right approach?
- Is there a better way to do it?
- Are they doing too much or too little?
- Is there too much detail or is it too succinct?
- Did they do too much research or too little?
- Are they working too quickly or too slowly?
- Are there resources that they aren't aware of?
- Is there someone they should speak to?

This kind of feedback will help your team members stay on track and feel like they are learning from you.

Which do you choose?

You've delegated a task and it comes back totally different from what you wanted. You:

a) Blast the person for being so stupid.

b) Say nothing and fix it yourself.

c) Review the work together and provide feedback on how to correct it, then commit to providing clearer instruction in future.

Do Not Micromanage

No one likes to be micromanaged. Think back to a job where someone was constantly looking over your shoulder or telling you exactly how to do something: you probably didn't appreciate it. When people are micromanaged, they are not as creative, they do not think for themselves, and they fail to learn the valuable lessons inherent in making their own mistakes. Worse, micromanaging blurs the understanding of who is accountable for the work. If you, as the boss, dictate every detail of how you want something done, the person doing it has not been empowered and will simply point at you if anything goes wrong. You still need to be aware of enough of the details to know what is going on and how it is progressing, but getting into the details cannot be at the expense of the other person. You do not want a situation where you cannot hold the person accountable because, in fact, you are doing her job. The person whom you micromanage will start thinking as soon as you stop doing it for her.

In order to delegate, you have to let go of control. This is not the easiest thing to do when you are a new manager. Delegation seems frightening, especially if you are concerned about looking like you are in charge. In your previous role, you may have had a lot of control over your work; however, in a management position, you have to influence people to get things done, as opposed to doing it for them. Influencing is a process of using your leadership skills to get things done through other people. Influencing requires motivation, communication of purpose and goals, ensuring that resources are available, removing barriers, and generating enthusiasm and excitement. It is a good idea to get feedback from your staff about the quantity of work being delegated to them. Do not be afraid to ask your team how you are doing in terms of empowering them to find solutions or completing their tasks in their own way. Although you do not want to micromanage, you also have to know when to go deep. That is, you need to know when to "go to where the truth is." In Japanese, the scene of a crime is called *gemba*, or the place where the truth is. Detectives need to go to *gemba* in order to determine what really happened. In your work, the place where the truth is will be wherever you can get the facts and wherever the source of the issue is. This might be talking with a particular person or going to the call centre or the manufacturing floor. You want to find the clues and take a look at what has happened or is happening in order to solve the issue or problem that has arisen. As you try to find the appropriate balance of accountability, empowerment, and delegation, seek feedback from your team and guidance from your boss.

Confront Issues

There's a saying: "What you permit, you promote." This is especially true in the workplace. Often one of the hardest things to do as a new manager is confront issues; it is much easier to avoid confrontation and conflict. There might be some part of you that hopes it will go away or sort itself out. This is an option (which might be appropriate in certain circumstance), but generally speaking, if you do not confront an issue, it will always come back to haunt you. You must have the courage to deal with issues head on. The first thing to do when you become aware of an issue is to gather the facts. This means spending time with all affected parties to understand the various sides to the issue, gather concrete statistics, and other information that is relevant. For example, if people are frequently absent, gathering the facts means getting data on when and how often they have been absent and whether they have sick notes, so that when you speak to them, you have concrete facts to refer to. If this is the first time that the issue has come up, you can start with expressing your concern. "Justin, I noticed you have been absent quite a bit, is there anything I can do to support you?" You will either get to a real issue or get an excuse. You can monitor the situation and see if it continues, at which time you can escalate the conversation: "Justin, I know this is the second time we are discussing your absenteeism. Your co-workers and I are relying on you to be here." Get help from your boss or your personnel department in terms of how to document this and how to proceed appropriately.

In addition to violations of organizational policies, which could include harassment, bullying, or improper use of email, you should also deal with behaviour that is inappropriate, such as callous or hurtful exchanges that you witness. In this regard, the values of your organization should provide a moral compass to use in the situation. For example, you could approach the person whose behaviour you want to deal with and say, "Do you feel that what you did is consistent with our value of [respect, dignity, dedication]?" Use your organizational values to confront issues. The conflicts and behaviours that are more difficult to put your finger on are the ones that are brewing or the ones that you are peripherally aware of. Take heed. The old adage, "Where there's smoke, there's fire" is absolutely true in workplaces. I remember being a supervisor and someone from another department made an offhand remark about one of my staff: "Don't worry, she has lots of time on her hands." I had no idea what this was about, but the comment lingered with me. I had a gut feeling that something was wrong, but did not know what it was. I decided to seek quantifiable measures of performance (and non-performance) for my entire department. I let the team know that I was seeking this information, in order to find opportunities for us to improve. I gathered information such as how many transactions each person was processing each month, industry comparators for workload, and the one item that became critical—I asked the technology department to run a summary of the websites that were most accessed by my department. It turned out that my staff member was on gaming sites several hours a day. Clearly this was against company policy, but also important was the impact her activity was having on other employees, who knew what was going on but feared saying anything. Be open and attuned to subtle or offhand remarks made by team members; look deeper into a concern or complaint that has come to your attention. Trust your gut instinct in these situations and follow through when you sense that something is wrong. It is important to be proactive. When you investigate a situation, be fair and open-minded, while working diligently to gather facts and data to understand the situation. Ask staff open-ended, candid questions so that you can get to the heart of the issue. Listen attentively, and have the inquisitiveness to go deeper. Ultimately, you are setting the example of what kind of environment is acceptable. The workplace should always be a place that is safe and free of inappropriate behaviour. You have a responsibility to take immediate action if something occurs that violates these principles.

Right Person, Right Job

You have the responsibility of ensuring that the right person is doing the right job. This goes back to what we said in an earlier chapter: that your most important job is to get the best out of people. When the right people are doing the right job, it is much easier to get the best from them. How do you know if the wrong person is doing the job? You might notice that the person is constantly complaining, not being a team player, or not being client-focused. The feedback may come from the person's colleagues, and clients, as well as your own observations. Perhaps the person is missing deadlines, demanding a lot of your time, or not meeting performance targets. You must deal with this. A performance review is a way to help the person see exactly what it is that you need her or him to change. This gives the person an opportunity to do so. If the person chooses not to change, or is not capable of changing, it is your job to terminate the relationship with the person. In my experience, the wrong person in a job negatively affects at least one other person. Help the person move on to something that will be a better fit. Your responsibility is to do what is best for the organization and this may not be what is best for an individual. One of my previous bosses taught me to hire slowly but fire quickly. It means make sure you take your time to hire the right person, but if you have the wrong person, let them go as quickly as possible.

What if you have the right person in the wrong job? This means that you have a person who is a good fit with the organization, or who you feel is talented and has potential, but the job the person has is not necessarily appropriate for her or him. In such cases, it is useful to discuss the situation directly with the person in order to determine what the person would prefer to be doing or where the person sees himself. Assuming you feel the person is right for another position, you would assist in seeking opportunities for him to move to another, more appropriate job within the organization. This is a great time to use your network in the organization to make connections for the person.

Be Supportive

It is important to be available for people and to let them know that you are there for them. Showing genuine concern for their work issues, needs, and interests will build both respect and trust. Being supportive in this case means building individual relationships, listening when people need to speak to you, having an open door policy, being flexible, and providing encouragement and ongoing feedback. Simply being considerate of others is an attribute that seems small, but can go a long way in creating harmony among your team members. Being considerate demonstrates concern and respect and is a tangible way to show support. Another way to be supportive is to understand your team members' interests in career and skill development. Giving people opportunities to take a course, chair a meeting, or lead an initiative is a wonderful ways to show that you care about their needs and want them to succeed.

Each staff member is unique, which is the real strength of a team. I often have to remind myself that people value their work differently; for example, not everyone wants to be a senior executive. Everyone's values or personal goals will be different, and usually will change over time. You can be supportive by being open to these different perspectives, while being true to your responsibilities to your organization. Another aspect of being supportive is remaining attuned to different staff styles in order to mould your approach to each person. You might consider how a person likes you to communicate with him and how often. Does the person prefer getting right to the facts or having time to socialize first? Being willing to adapt to your staff will send a clear message of support that significantly enhances your relationship.

(i) *www.inspireyourcareer.com*

Inspire Your Career Tips

- Create a vision of what you want to accomplish.
- Ensure each team member is clear on her or his role and responsibilities.
- Set measurable, achievable performance expectations for individuals and the team as a whole.
- Check in with how people are doing and provide feed back on their work.
- Delegate to your staff: be clear on what they need to do, not how to do it.
- Be courageous and confront issues head on.
- Be supportive by moulding your style to accommodate individuals.
- Create a positive work environment.

CHAPTER 11
Building a Great Team

"Teamwork is the ability to work together toward a common vision. It is the fuel that allows common people to attain uncommon results."
Andrew Carnegie

I love Robert Fulghum's list from *All I Really Need to Know I Learned in Kindergarten*. The points are delightful and entirely applicable to working in a team:

- Share everything;
- Play fair;
- Clean up your own mess;
- Don't take things that aren't yours;
- Say you're sorry when you hurt somebody;
- When you go out into the world...stick together;
- Be aware of wonder.

What binds these lessons together are themes of respect and appreciation for others. These are the qualities that make good teams great. When individuals come together to accomplish a task or goal, and they are bound together by a deep appreciation for what others are bringing to the table and respect for others' opinions and ideas, the team will flourish and success is the result. Your goal as the manager is to create a team culture of mutual respect and appreciation, one in which there is palpable harmony within and between relationships, where new information can easily be processed, and where there is excellent execution of team responsibilities.

To accomplish this, your job is part cheerleader, part ringleader, and part coach. You want to create the conditions that will allow the team to reach its fullest potential. You need to be able to inspire, empower, and motivate people to genuinely want to work together to create a successful team. You want them to feel that they are part of something larger than themselves; that together, you can achieve more. In this chapter, we will focus on several aspects of how to create a great team.

Set Goals Together

Your team's job is to help the organization do what it sets out to accomplish, while being true to its values and mission. In order to accomplish this, your team needs to know and understand the organization's strategic plan and objectives for the coming year. In addition, depending on your role in the organization, it might be valuable to obtain other types of data to share with your team, such as client satisfaction information for your area, performance indicator data, or financial information. You might also consider inviting your boss, the financial officer, or another appropriate person to speak to your team about the strategic plan. This has the added benefit of connecting your team to more senior members of the organization.

Your role is to lead the team in setting goals that are aligned with the organization's strategic plan and objectives. There a number of ways to set team goals. You could have a team retreat somewhere away from the office. You could have a longer than usual meeting where you use brainstorming techniques to determine what goals the team would like to achieve. You could do a SWOT analysis—identifying Strengths, Weaknesses, Opportunities, and Threats with the team—from which goals can emerge. You could solicit feedback from your team through a survey or conduct a focus group with a mix of staff and clients.

(i) *www.inspireyourcareer.com*

Whatever method you choose to solicit input for goal setting, the important thing is to engage your team in this process. If you try to create your team's goals alone or in collaboration with only your boss, you will have missed a huge opportunity to engage your team and get participation and support from them on the direction that you are going. If they did not take part in this valuable exercise, the team goals are remote and unconnected to them. The process of bringing a team together to develop goals is, in and of itself, a team-building exercise. It is one of the best ways to create focus and clarity for your team about where you are going, what the priorities are, and what they are accountable for.

Give People a Cause

I worked as a senior vice-president in a hospital and was responsible for a large renovation. As part of the renovation, we had to move 300 frail patients from one part of the hospital to another. When I gathered a large, multi-disciplinary, multi-departmental working group together to plan out this complex move, I told them the story of my dad, who earlier that year had been in palliative care with cancer. He was moved from one room to another—something that may not sound like a big deal at all. But at that point, all he had left were the small things that mattered to him, the pictures and cards pinned to the bulletin board and personal items on his end table. No one in the family was told about the move, and none of us were there when it happened. When we got there later that day, he was a complete wreck, upset and very disoriented because his things were not where they were supposed to be. He died about a week later. Obviously the move didn't kill him, but it had a significant effect on the quality of his life for that very precious day. Telling this story to the hospital group inspired incredible creativity and a 100% patient-focused plan. Everyone worked as a team to ensure that the move went off brilliantly, with a 97% satisfaction level from our patients.

When people feel that what they do at work matters, the sense of fulfillment is palpable. When you can articulate the reason for doing the project and the actual end result of the work that your team is doing, it connects your team members to something meaningful. It connects them to a bigger picture and gives them a cause. If that bigger picture is full of numbers, facts, and figures, you won't get the same impact. What motivates and inspires people are human connections. If you can connect what your team is trying to achieve to something that makes a difference for people, your team will be hooked. This is also true at an individual level. When you are able to link a human connection to an individual's role, you link them to a greater reason for being. Answer for your team "Why is what we're doing important?" and "Why does it matter?" Use opportunities to link what your team is doing, to things that matter. This will greatly motivate your team to do the very best it can.

Seek Diversity

One aspect to having a strong team is to ensure there is enough diversity of different ideas, perspectives, and opinions. Having a homogenous group can easily lead to "groupthink" where everyone is nodding in agreement to what others say. A diverse team has a high level of creative potential and simply needs support and guidance to allow that potential to flourish. Consider diversity in the broadest sense of the term. It includes geographic, cultural, and gender diversity, as well as experience, skill, and personality diversity.

You will likely inherit the team you have when you start as the team lead or manager, so there is not a lot you can initially do with the makeup of the team. However, you can be conscious of the makeup of the team; for example, does the team represent the customers or market you serve? Does your team adequately represent the geography it serves? Is your team full of new people or people with lots of experience? Understanding the composition of your team is helpful as you try to accomplish your objectives. Where you have an opportunity to put a work group or task force together, consider how you can create a diverse group. You may, for example, look for a mix of new and experienced staff, a mix of people who work in different geographies, and a mix of personality types. You can include those who are conservative along with people who are risk takers. Energetic people could be represented alongside those who would be considered passive. The strength of tapping into these various perspectives is that you will tap into the richness within the organization and draw out the diverse lenses through which people look to interpret information.

Let Creativity and Innovation Flow

I am always amazed at what can happen when you bring a group together to work on a common goal. With the right conditions, the individuals become a community. They listen to each other, they build on what others say, and brilliant ideas emerge. Creating the environment for a team's natural wisdom, insight, and creativity to emerge is a revered skill. In order for this kind of environment to exist, people need to feel that it is safe to bring forward new ideas, that they can take risks, and that there is an appetite and appreciation for innovation. You may work in an organization where this type of culture is firmly entrenched. You may work in an organization where it is pitifully lacking. What you can do, regardless of the organization, is work to influence and encourage this environment in your own team.

How can you create a culture of creativity and innovation? Encourage, recognize, and reward it. This sends a clear message that you want people to think, be creative, and bring ideas forward. The recognition and rewards do not have to be big—think of cheap and cheerful ways to say thank you and encourage new thinking. You can try to improve the structure you work in to support innovation. For example, if no new ideas ever get implemented because of the thick hierarchy in your organization, find ways to work around the barriers. You can discuss the issue with your boss while at the same time making it possible for ideas to be implemented within your team. You should consider at least one regular annual opportunity for brainstorming and out-of-the-box thinking. Ideally, this would be a retreat or some other forum where people are free from their day-to-day responsibilities and can be in a new atmosphere that allows ideas and dialogue to flow. As part of your role, there will also be opportunities to find efficiencies in your area of responsibility, which are also a form of innovation. For example, can you reduce expenses in some way? Can a process be improved? Can repetitive tasks be removed? Is there an opportunity to automate and find savings? As a manager, you will also have a role in supporting organization-wide innovation initiatives and being a role model of innovative thinking. Building and supporting a creative and innovative culture will allow your team to fulfill its potential.

Team Check-In

It is always a good idea to check in with your team members on how the team is performing. The idea is to try to determine how the members of the team are relating to the collective. For example, do they feel they are working well together? Is the team communicating? Does everyone have a say? Is the team reaching its full potential? This kind of check-in will bring to the surface practical things like changing the frequency or length of meetings or how you communicate with them. Ideally, checking in with your team will allow the more subtle, personal issues to emerge. These are the kinds of issues that can have devastating effects on team performance. For example, checking in may uncover that people feel uncomfortable speaking their mind, that they do not think they can be completely honest, or that they do not feel everyone is doing their fair share. This kind of feedback gives you a lot to work with, and once it does surface, you can work with your team to find the ways to resolve whatever issues have come up. Just by providing the opportunity for feedback on how the team is doing will set the stage for developing an open, collegial team.

If you are concerned that you will not hear from everyone, you could try a talking circle. The talking circle is an aboriginal tradition and is a great way to ensure that everyone has a say in a particular discussion. Once seated, you ask each person to give her or his thoughts, in this case, to the question "How is our team doing?" You can start with one person, who is holding a talking stick (or something more practical). While that person is speaking, no one else is allowed to speak. When she or he is finished, they pass the talking stick to the next person. This continues until you have heard from everyone. If your team has simmering issues and you feel it needs some anonymity to provide honest feedback, you could do a short survey. The survey, using a scale of one to five, could ask questions such as "How is the team doing?" and "How do you think it could be doing?" You could also ask open-ended questions such as "What suggestions do you have for reaching our full potential?" Collecting feedback from your team on a periodic basis lets everyone know that you care about what is going on within the team. Acting on the feedback you receive will help you reach your team's greatest potential.

Communicate (and Communicate Some More)

You have heard this said before, but it bears repeating: You can never communicate your message enough. Most messages are lost or forgotten or not clearly understood after the first time around. It is important to use multiple media to communicate and ensure you get feedback from your team as to what works. Establish a pattern of communication with your team, and coordinate this with whatever is happening corporately. You should consider newsletters, group emails, group voice mails, a suggestion box, or chat room. People want stability from their workplace and good communication establishes an underlying level of quality and constancy to people's work lives. People want to be in the loop and know what is going on locally and within the organization as a whole. Meetings are the other important component of communication. Consider whether you need to organize regular one-on-one meetings, small groups, or regular team meetings. You need to consider whom you need to meet with, how often, where, when, and for what purpose. Bringing your team together as a whole is very important, primarily so that they have a chance to physically be in the same room together. Establish this quickly once you have taken on your new role so that there is a regular team meeting time that people can book into their schedules. In addition to the regular agenda at team meetings, it's great to include some social time. The dynamics of your environment will dictate how you sort out the logistics for your team.

Although this seems counter-intuitive, one-on-one meetings are essential in building a great team. In all my years in management, one of the biggest complaints I hear is that people do not have enough time with their boss. This is voiced in many ways, for example, that their boss is always busy, that their boss is unavailable, or that their boss does not have an open door policy. Without one-on-one meetings, there is no opportunity for you to discuss an individual's work, provide feedback, and answer questions. If individuals feel they are important and being listened to, they will contribute more in the team environment. Having an open door policy also supports the development of both the individuals and the team because they feel you are there for them and they feel supported. Doing a periodic walk around is a great way to show your presence to staff. Literally walk around wherever your team is working. It is amazing what you pick up from just seeing things for yourself. People are in their own environment, so they tend to feel more confident and it is easier to have an informal chat. In addition, this kind of presence from a manager speaks volumes about what you think is important.

Reflection Exercise

Who do you need to communicate with at work?

What are the various ways that you communicate now?

Is your communication effective? Can you do better? How?

Team Referee

One of your jobs is to be the referee for your team. There are often behaviours that occur within a team environment that, while they do not necessarily contradict a particular policy, are detrimental to the smooth operation of the team and the work that the team is doing. It is sometimes tricky to know in these situations if something serious has occurred or if it was just a joke, whether you need to step in or let the parties sort it out, and what the appropriate response is. Here are some examples of team dynamics that you can watch out for:

- Team members who do not play fair: they leave their work for others to finish or never take on new projects.
- Team members who pick fights: they always seem to be in conflict with others or have aggressive tendencies.
- Team members who hog the ball: they keep information to themselves at the expense of others or pick the best or easiest work.
- Team members who yell at the referee: they always think they're right, and are never happy with your decisions or what is going on.
- Team members who complain from the sidelines: they love to whine about everything and anything.

Your role as team referee is to monitor these dynamics and know when to step in. You do not want to lose what is unique and different about the people you have, but on the other hand, you do not want the spirit and energy of your team to be damaged by the behaviour of a few people. In order to have a high performance team, you need to deal with behaviours that negatively impact the good of the whole. The way you do this will vary from person to person and from situation to situation. You might simply try reflecting back to the person what she is doing and how it influences others. You might incorporate the issue into the person's performance review. You might try to work with the issue in a team dynamic. Find the way that will best address the issue. Your team members will appreciate you stepping in when it is necessary.

Which do you choose?
Someone on your team always speaks up and has her say. You:

a) Do nothing.

b) Focus on trying to get quieter members of the team to speak.

c) Speak to the person privately, thank her for her enthusiasm, and suggest that at the next meeting she try to listen to others more.

Have Fun

People will always appreciate a leader who is enthusiastic, has fun, and who can laugh at herself. These are very positive, uplifting qualities that make a dramatic difference in the workplace. If you create a culture where team members laugh, have fun, and enjoy their time together, the quality of their work life will go up exponentially. When people are happy at work, they have a sense of balance and feel good about what they are doing. Even if you are a quiet, reserved person, you can still encourage an enjoyable workplace environment. You can consider asking one of your team members to assist or lead in planning fun activities. Normally, there is a natural social convener who would be perfect for this role.

Ideally, you can incorporate a positive atmosphere into everything you do. But with the speed that workplaces operate in, this can be tough. It is a good idea to plan periodic fun events for your team. You will have your own ideas based on the culture of your organization and the interests of your team, but here are a few to get you started:

- Enter your team in a charity fundraiser,
- Have a potluck lunch,
- Organize an education session over lunch ("Lunch & Learn"),
- Play Pictionary or charades,
- Start a book club,
- Exchange recipes,
- Watch a funny video together,
- Go bowling together,
- Organize a "Clean Up Friday"; order in lunch and give your team time to clean up their office, their computer files, and their emails.

Of course, do not forget the importance of genuinely appreciating your team. Recognize and reward your team as much as possible in order to support the positive work environment that you are trying to create.

Inspire Your Career Tips
- Set goals as a team.
- Give people a meaningful reason to do their job.
- Encourage creativity and innovation.
- Have your team evaluate itself regarding how it is doing.
- Deal with inappropriate behaviour confidently, swiftly, and professionally.
- Communicate frequently using different media.
- Laugh, have fun, and appreciate your team.

CHAPTER 12
From Conflict to Calm

"Holding on to anger is like grasping a hot coal with the intent of throwing it at someone else; you are the one who gets burned."
Buddha

Conflict is everywhere. We experience it in all facets of our life; we see it in our families, our social circles, our workplace, and our world. Conflict will always exist. We are all human beings, with our unique backgrounds, opinions, and ways of doing things. We bring these unique perspectives into every conversation, every exchange, and every relationship with other human beings. Inevitably, we will have situations where the perspective we bring is completely different from another person's. What we have power over, what can transform a situation from conflict to calm, is our reaction to these different perspectives. Ask yourself, "How do I react to a view that is entirely different from my own?" and "What actions and words will I choose to deal with conflict with my partner, my family, my boss, or the driver who just cut me off in traffic?" Instead of eliminating conflict, which is impossible, we can focus on eliminating the aggressive, hurtful, poisonous words and actions that often erupt when our perspective clashes with that of others.

Conflicts at Work

Conflicts at work can occur in many forms. We may have a one-time conflict with someone that relates to a specific issue or situation. We may also have ongoing conflicts with someone we work with. This can occur because of conflicts in personality, in values, in work habits, all kinds of things. There are also conflicts that will happen on an ongoing basis in any work environment. Here are a few examples of things that can cause conflict in a workplace:

- Tension between making money and providing more service,
- Legislative or regulatory requirements,
- Choices between what to invest in (e.g. product, service, capital),
- Tension between reducing risks and being cost effective,
- Choices made during economic downturns or economic booms,
- Tension between disadvantaging one group while another is given an advantage.

You must be able to handle conflict, particularly when we consider the many ways that it occurs in a work environment e.g. interpersonal, situational, and external. Work is an ongoing, daily activity. Stress created by fractious relationships and tense situations, when left unchecked, will grow in magnitude and intensity over time. The weight of these difficult relationships and situations spreads beyond the people directly involved to others in the work area. Like a bad cold, once conflict takes hold it makes you feel worse, it infects others you are in contact with, and it is really hard to shake. Take responsibility for the conflict that you create or fuel in your workplace and commit to transforming conflict to calm.

Fear Triggers and Taking Responsibility

Before we discuss practical approaches to dealing with conflict, there are two very important points that need to be understood and accepted. The first is that we have triggers that quickly move us into conflict. We will call these "fear triggers." Everyone has fear triggers. What most people do not have is an understanding of what their own fear triggers are. Without this basic understanding of what triggers conflict for you, it is difficult to get to the root of how to resolve it. The second point is that we are responsible for our words and actions. The deflection of accountability for our words and actions is a significant contributor to conflict. Let's discuss these further.

"Why is this a conflict for me?" This is a great question to ask yourself. Why is this person, this action, or this situation creating a negative reaction? Generally, when a situation occurs at work, it becomes a conflict because you feel that the situation negatively affects you. You feel threatened, that you are going to lose something, that you will have to do something you do not want to do, or that your worth or image is being compromised. At the root of conflict is fear, and that fear comes from within you. As soon as the fear is triggered, strong emotions rise up and strategically place themselves throughout your body. Your heart beats faster. Your face turns red. Your head pounds. Your stomach ties itself into a knot. Your eyes water. Your breathing quickens. And that is only what is going on with your body. Your mind also picks up the pace, zooming from thought to thought, playing out various scenarios based on the situation. Your mind and your body feel out of control. What are your fear triggers?

- Are you afraid of losing control?
- Are you afraid of not being liked?
- Are you afraid of criticism?
- Are you afraid of losing prestige?
- Are you afraid of being wrong?
- Are you afraid of being vulnerable?
- Are you afraid that you are not good enough?

Being human means we all have fears that trigger certain responses and that are at the root of conflict. Understanding what your fear triggers are will help you better deal with conflict.

Who is responsible for your words and actions? You are. You are responsible for your words and actions. This may sound trite, but let's really think about it. Think back to the last argument or the last time you became angry and upset with someone. In that moment, who was responsible for your actions and words? Your first reaction, if you're honest, will be to say the other person. It was her fault that I could not get my work done. Why can't he be more organized? Can't she see I am right? Blaming others can continue indefinitely if you do not take responsibility for your contribution. Even if you do not verbalize the blame, it goes through your mind. The first thing you need to admit and accept is that you are responsible for your words and actions. This is critical; it means that regardless of the facts of the situation and regardless of how much you can justify your position, you accept that the words coming out of your mouth and any actions that follow are conscious choices that you are making. Remember this as we start to look at how to transform conflict.

How Do I Deal with Conflict?

Most of us do not like being in a conflict for too long. It drains our energy and does not feel particularly good. There are a few personality types who revel in confrontation, but a constant barrage of conflict will wear down even these individuals. So in a broad, general way, you want to approach any and every conflict with a desire to be of help, not harm. I am going to present several ideas on how to deal with conflict, through different approaches to a single, simple scenario. I believe that in dealing with conflict, it is best to have a large toolbox filled with different ways of handling a situation. You can try the different approaches, use multiple approaches in the same situation, or combine approaches. The idea is to experiment with the different tools to see what works for you.

Let's look at a scenario:

Your boss asked for a volunteer to set up a display table at a conference. You volunteer and set up the display. Your colleague Ann looks at your work and says it looks awful. Ann sat silently during the meeting when the boss originally asked for volunteers.

Approach 1: Pause and reflect

What is your immediate reaction to the scenario above? Depending on your personality, you may instantly get your back up and get angry, "How dare she say that? Who does she think she is?" You might wither away, wondering, "What did I do wrong? I am so useless." You might take the comment personally, "Why doesn't she like me?" or "How did I offend her?" Whatever your reaction is, just pause and reflect on it. Ideally, if you can do this for a moment before you respond, your response may change dramatically from your first instinct. If you have already reacted to the person's comment, you can still take the time to pause and reflect afterwards. Which fear triggers lit up in that moment that you were criticized?

You can also use the "Five Whys" that we talked about in the Knowing your Blind Spots chapter to dig deeper into the root cause of your reaction.

Approach 2: Be inquisitive

You can ask Ann questions to better understand her point of view. There is always another side to a story and another way to look at things. Be inquisitive. Ask, "What exactly don't you like Ann?" and "How would you have done it differently?" "Why do you feel so strongly about the way it is set up?" The idea here is to be genuinely curious about why the person feels the way they do and to be interested and open to another way of doing things. Sometimes just letting the other person be heard is all it takes to diffuse the situation.

Approach 3: Collaborate

In this approach, you can acknowledge the person's strong feelings and try to come up with a way to accommodate her ideas. For example, you could say, "I see this really matters to you Ann, let's discuss how we can make the display look better." Have an open discussion about your different opinions so that you can try to come to a solution that takes the best ideas from each of you. This approach also requires a willingness to hear and an openness to appreciate other ideas.

Approach 4: Acknowledge and let go

Here you are able to listen to the other person without judgment or projection into the situation. You simply acknowledge the person's comment and completely let it go. You might say for example, "Thanks for stopping by Ann, I appreciate the feedback."

Approach 5: Compromise

A compromise can be useful in dealing with conflict, particularly if the benefits of doing so outweigh the cost. In our scenario, if maintaining a good relationship with your colleague is ultimately more important than hanging on to your way of setting up the display, it would be worth giving something up. Let Ann redo some element of the display. Please note that the key to compromise is to compromise and let go, not compromise and resent. Compromising and resenting the other person will eat away at you and probably worsen the situation. If you hold on to the resentment, the next interaction with this person will be worse than it needs to be. Compromising and letting go allows you to keep your sense of self, without great attachment to the thing or object of the conflict.

Approach 6: Empathize and Redirect

In the moment that Ann made her remark, you can recognize that she is feeling threatened. You can feel her fear trigger rise up. Ann may feel threatened that you are going to get more recognition from your boss and that she will be forgotten. Instead of focusing on what is going on with you, connect to what is going on with her. You could actually feel a sense of camaraderie because you both want to do a good job and be successful. In the instant of confrontation, you can appreciate and truly feel what Ann is going through, and you empathize. Empathy requires an extension of kindness to the other person. A great way to verbalize empathy (assuming you mean it) is to say things like, "I appreciate how you are feeling." The next step is to redirect the person to an alternative, to another person, or to a next step. In our scenario, you could say, "I value your input on this, perhaps we could talk further in the office tomorrow."

Reflection Exercise

Describe a recent situation where there was conflict between you and someone else.

_____

_____

_____

Upon reflection, what triggered the conflict for you? What triggered your fear?

_____

_____

_____

Choose one of the approaches above and apply it to your conflict. How would the outcome have changed?

_____

_____

_____

Dealing with Abuse

Another form of conflict that can arise is abuse. This might include harassment, bullying, or discrimination. Abuse can take many forms, but generally the perpetrator's behaviour has the effect of degrading, humiliating, or intimidating the other person. Abuse has no place in a workplace (or anywhere for that matter). Most organizations have policies related to abuse. Many provincial and state laws exist to protect individuals in workplace abuse situations—check your jurisdiction. If you are a victim of abuse in your workplace, the first step is to follow your organization's policies and procedures. This might include informing your boss, documenting the situation, or writing a formal complaint. In cases where the abuse is from a client or customer, and dealing with clients or customers is part of your job, you should have appropriate tools and training to defuse the situation and redirect the abuser. You should also be able to seek support from your employer when abuse from a client or customer occurs.

When the abuse is not blatant, when it has formed part of the culture, or when it is coming from a superior, it can be difficult to find a clear solution to what to do. The power dynamics can be very difficult to navigate. Here are some examples:

- You are the only male teacher in a primary school. You are the object of many jokes and sexual innuendos.
- A workplace mentor, who is not your boss, seems to be getting too comfortable in the relationship. Personal questions are coming up more and more often.
- Your boss is a bully and constantly puts you down, especially in front of others.

What can you do? It is important to document everything that is happening, both to protect yourself and to build your case if required. The behaviour should be addressed directly with the person responsible. This can be difficult, but the person needs to know that he or she has crossed a boundary with you. I read of a situation where a person recorded another person yelling at her and then played it back to the person yelling. This had both an instant and ongoing effect, forcing the person to consider their behaviour and, possibly, changing the person's tendency to yell at others. You should read and understand any company policies that exist on abuse and follow the procedures indicated. You can go to your personnel department and get advice. If the abuser is not your boss, you need to speak to your boss about the situation. If the abuser is your boss, in addition to the personnel department, you might consider getting advice from someone who is a peer to your boss. This has the added benefit of making another person who is at the same level as the abuser aware of the situation. Ultimately, you will need to decide if you can remain in the situation, if you can change the situation, or if you need to leave the situation.

(i) *www.inspireyourcareer.com*

Know When to Walk Away

There is a line in Kenny Rogers's song "The Gambler": "You gotta know when to hold 'em, know when to fold 'em, know when to walk away, know when to run." Throughout your career, there will be situations that draw out strong emotional reactions from you. Perhaps you are incensed over a decision that is made, exasperated by the work habits of a colleague, or infuriated with a barrier to your progress. Situations that solicit strong reactions are often ones where we do not have control over what is happening. There may be a strong sense of resentment towards one or more people for their involvement in the situation. We may also feel a sense of injustice or inequity about what happened. You need to use your judgment to navigate what to do. You can use the techniques described above to help you defuse the conflict. You might take other steps such as discussing the situation with your boss, human resources, or an external resource. Notwithstanding the desire to resolve or bring equity or justice to the situation, it is really important to know when to stop. Often we are not in the position to escalate or resolve an issue. Perhaps we do not have the authority or power. The problem may simply not be ours to solve because it is not our responsibility. The issue may also not be solvable due to the culture or leadership of the organization.

Let's look at an example:

Diana's project has gone completely sideways because her teammate Lisa, who reports to the same boss, did not finish an important aspect of the project. Diana is furious and wants Lisa to be held accountable and bear the consequences of her lack of performance. Diana has a few options. She can speak to her boss about the situation or she can speak to Lisa about the situation. She may even speak to human resources about the situation. But ultimately, the situation may not get resolved, or may not be resolved to Diana's satisfaction. Diana is not in control of her boss and she has no direct control over her colleague. There will be a point where Diana has to simply let go of the situation and her emotional connection to it.

Part of your career development will involve learning when to pursue an issue and knowing when to walk away.

How Can I Stay Calm?

Staying calm during a conflict is desirable because it helps you, physically and emotionally, it helps the other person, and it helps the work environment overall. Your ability to stay calm is like a pebble dropped in the pond; the ripple effect is certain and immediate. Calm radiates out and helps others be calm. We can probably think of people in our lives who have a calming effect on us. The opposite is also true: anger hurts you, physically and emotionally, it hurts the other person, and it hurts the work environment. Anger never creates a stable situation. In all my years of work, I cannot think of a single example where an outburst, or yelling or screaming at another person, was justified. It never is. Staying calm is something that you can work on and improve over time.

Which do you choose?

You are steaming mad at a co-worker. You:

a) *Yell at her.*
b) *Fire off an email about how you feel.*
c) *Take three deep breaths, pause, and reflect on why you*

are so upset. When you're calm, speak to her about what happened.

The approaches to conflict described in the section above are helpful tools for staying calm in a situation. Here are a few additional tips to try:

- *Have a good intention.* When faced with a conflict, ask yourself, "What can I do to help this situation?" Having an intention to make things better will put your mind in a different, more helpful place. If it is too difficult to be this positive, you can at least have the intention of not making the situation worse. When your mind is aligned to positive intentions, the actions that follow have a better chance of being positive.

- *Breathe.* Breathing is powerful, simple, highly effective, and always available. Before you respond to a person whom you think has slighted you, before you hit "send" on that fuming email, before you complain to someone about a person who has wronged you, take one deep breath. Take another deep breath. Take a third deep breath. Your outlook will have completely changed.

- *Respond, don't react.* Usually, we have an instant desire to react to conflict. Reacting has a quality of strong emotion to it, while responding has a quality of rationality and thoughtfulness to it. Learn to respond to conflict versus reacting to it.

- *Use humour.* Humour is a fabulous way to defuse conflict. It can lighten up a tense situation and create more space. We can probably all remember an uneasy situation where someone said something funny that made everyone laugh and cleared the air.

- *"It's not about me."* When confronted with conflict, say this phrase in your head. It will help redirect your energy away from your immediate emotions. It allows you, in that second, to detach what just happened from your emotional reaction to it. You can start to see these are two separate parts of the conflict: the words and actions that caused the conflict and your emotional reaction to them. You may not have control over the cause of the conflict, but you do have control over how you react.

- *Stay open.* This means keeping your mind and heart open. If your mind can stay open, there is a better chance of saying the right thing, of seeing alternative solutions, and of making the best out of the situation. If your heart can stay open, there is a better chance of feeling kindness towards the other person, even if you do not like what she said or did. As your mind and heart close, so will your ability to transform the situation from conflict to calm. Believe that much of what you feel is within your control and can be shaped to achieve a different outcome.

Inspire Your Career Tips
- Know what your fear triggers are.
- Take responsibility for your words and actions.
- Experiment with tools such as "Pause and reflect," "Acknowledge and let go," and "Empathize and redirect" to deal with conflict.
- Have the intention of not making a conflict worse.
- Take three deep breaths when you need to feel calm.
- Use humour to defuse a tense situation.

CHAPTER 13
Finding Balance

"Happiness is not a matter of intensity but of balance and order and rhythm and harmony."
Thomas Merton

In our techno-rich, fast-paced society, it is essential to consciously and purposefully make choices that will help you stay balanced, healthy, and happy. Finding and maintaining balance in your life will result in a sense of fulfillment and joy where you can feel confident and in control of your life. Work-life balance means finding harmony between time spent working and time spent in other aspects of your life. Achieving balance in your life is not easy; it is a lot of work. It requires awareness about what is going on in your life, what you are happy about, and whether you are where you want to be. It requires resolve and discipline in order to change the things you want to change and to make those changes sustainable in your life. In this chapter, we'll discuss various aspects of achieving balance in your life, personally and professionally.

Evaluate Your Life

A key aspect of work-life balance is that its definition is up to you; you determine what the "balance" or "equality" is. Only you can decide what is important to you and what you need do to feel fulfilled. Your answer will be completely different from the person next to you. So the first step is to take stock of your life. Try recording where you spend your time during one week. How many hours do you spend at work, how many with family or friends, watching television, or reading? Knowing how much time you spend on various activities will give you a baseline of what the components of your life are right now. Then write down all the things that are important to you and how much time you would like to spend on each. Take a look at your two lists: the one with the things you are doing now and the one with what you would like to be doing. The gaps will be evident. You will see what you are spending time on that is not important and the things that are important, but that you do not have time for. You can now work towards realigning your life with your true priorities.

Let's work on an example. Assuming that in a week, you sleep an average of eight hours a day and let's take off a few hours a day for getting ready, etc., there are approximately 98 hours left in one week. Here's what an analysis might look like:

What I Do Now	Time Per Week	What I Would Like to Do
Work	40 hours	40 hours
Commute	10 hours	5 hours
Hang out with friends	8 hours	9 hours
Cook/Eat	10 hours	10 hours
Clean	3 hours	3 hours
Spend time with family	6 hours	7 hours
Watch TV	10 hours	7 hours
Read	2 hours	2 hours
Exercise	5 hours	6 hours
Computer/Video Games	4 hours	3 hours
Learn a language		2 hours
Spiritual activity		2 hours
Volunteer		2 hours
Total	98 hours	98 hours

ⓘ www.inspireyourcareer.com

In the example above, there is a desire to reduce the commute time. This may require negotiating working one day from home, or from an office that is situated closer to you. The point is that you have articulated your desire to reduce the time involved in this activity. You have acknowledged that this is important to you. You will also note in our example that we have added a number of new activities that we previously did not have time for—learning a language, spiritual activity, and volunteering. In order to add these, we had to reduce time spent in other areas. The benefits of this exercise are not so much in the end result, but in the process of really looking at where your time is being spent and reflecting on what you would like to change in order to add more quality to your life.

By quantifying time spent in your weekly routine, you have a more accurate and unbiased reflection of what is currently happening in order to move to your desired state.

Evaluating your life is something that should be done periodically. Life is not static; it continually evolves and changes. There may be times where you need to pause and re-evaluate your priorities. For example, when you get married, have children, or get a promotion. Life also has a habit of throwing you lots of curve balls, which are unexpected, unplanned, and not within your control. You may have to look at your life differently and re-evaluate what balance means when a significant event takes place like having to suddenly care for a sick parent, a death in your family, or getting fired from your job. These kinds of significant, unplanned events require you to consider how you are going to balance multiple priorities. Evaluating your life is also an excellent idea whenever you are feeling unsettled, melancholy, or unhappy. These feelings can be a message that something is missing in your life. Stop to take stock of what is going on and think about what it is that you really want. Don't be afraid to pause in order to reflect on what adjustments need to be made to help you achieve more balance and greater happiness.

Give Yourself Permission

Some people will have no problem with giving themselves permission to make changes to their lives. They will look at the lists they made above and immediately make adjustments. For others, it is more difficult. We all know people who find it hard to put themselves ahead of others. It is easy for them to relegate themselves to last on the list of people who need to be taken care of. If you feel you do not deserve to take care of yourself or that someone or something else is always more important than you are, you will never achieve work-life balance. You are the most important component of your life. And yes, others need and rely on you, but they can only benefit from what you have to offer when you are at your best, when you are your healthiest physically, mentally, and emotionally. Ultimately you are the architect of your life and you are making choices every day about what it looks like.

Three other aspects of giving yourself permission are:

- giving yourself permission to say no;

- giving yourself permission to set boundaries; and
- giving yourself permission to stop doing things.

Saying no can be difficult or awkward, so most of us do not like to do it. This can lead to feeling burdened by something or someone, because we are not being true to how we are feeling about the situation. For example, you may have a friend who loves to talk; she calls you constantly and takes up a lot of your time. You are feeling burdened by this but do not know what to do. Giving yourself permission to say no means being honest and saying you do not want to be on the phone so much. It is fairly easy to become completely over-scheduled and over-committed, which means no down time and fewer hours to do some of the basic necessities of caring for yourself and your family.

Setting parameters is another option that can allow you to gracefully manage demands for your time. In the situation above, for example, you could tell your friend that she cannot call you until after 8 p.m. You can set parameters when you accept a commitment; for example, by limiting the time commitment to a certain number of hours per month or limiting the duration of your involvement. Setting parameters can also be done on a life scale. My brother and sister-in-law for example, decided to reorganize their lives so that one of them was always home with their kids. They reduced their cost of living, my sister-in-law took a part-time nursing position, and my brother booked chiropody patients only two and a half days a week. They consciously restructured their lives around what mattered most to them.

Finally, take a look at what you can stop doing. Ask yourself, "What is consuming my time and adding little or no value?" You might go back to the list you made and realize that you spend a lot of time on the computer or playing video games, but not enough time exercising. You can decide if there are some things you can stop doing in order to allow more time for other activities. There might be a person or people in your life who you want to spend less time with. Again, although this may be awkward, it is important to address in order to enhance your quality of life.

Make It Happen

Evaluating your life is a great start. Taking your thoughts and ideas and making them real requires you to act. It's the "doing" that will take things out of the realm of a wish or a dream and place them into reality. If in your assessment of your life you want to travel, making it a reality requires action. The "doing" might include assessing the financial implications of the trip, developing an itinerary, and planning the time off. You need to take steps to achieve your goal. In our travel example, you may need to work extra hours for a while or save more than usual each month. You may need to be creative about how you travel and where you stay. You may need to work out special arrangements at work. You will need discipline to actually execute your plan so that your trip becomes a reality. Action requires your will, creativity, and discipline. Do not let dreams get stuck in your head, indefinitely. If something is really important to you, then do it. Use your ingenuity to come up with the options and solutions that will get you to where you need to be.

Which do you choose?

You are working full-time, but want to travel to Europe. You:
a) Quit your job and go.
b) Go during your two weeks of vacation.
c) Present a plan to your boss to go during the slowest month at work, taking two weeks of vacation and two weeks unpaid leave of absence.

Implementing your plans, while balancing what is possible with your work, will be another consideration. You may have a workplace that is very supportive of work-life balance and has the related policies, programs, and activities in place. You may have a workplace where the culture does not support work-life balance. Whatever the situation is, if your action plan requires some change with your work situation, you can always ask. For example, if the evaluation of your life leads you to a goal of working fewer hours, contemplate what options you could present to your boss in order to make this happen. You may want to ask to work part-time or to job share or work one day a week from home. Consider what might be possible and prepare a good case, anticipating all the possible concerns. Other options you could consider include, taking an unpaid leave of absence, taking days off without pay, or asking for a reassignment to a different role. Again, be creative in trying to get to where you want to be.

A final point on making it easier to make the important things happen in your life is to ensure that you are as efficient as possible. This is particularly true of the things in your life that must be done but are more mundane. Consider these tips for saving time in order to create more space in your life:

- Can you reduce time travelling between tasks by using services that are closer to either your work or your home?
- Can you run errands on your lunch hour?
- Can you reduce your commute or use transit?
- Is there anything you would be willing to pay to get done, e.g. hiring a cleaner?
- Are places you frequent often close to your home or work, e.g. grocery store, gym, health services, dry cleaning?

Attitude Adjustment

We have talked about attitude in relation to being successful in the workplace. Your attitude also makes a huge difference in what becomes stressful in your life and how well you are able to handle career and personal pressures. If you have a negative, pessimistic attitude, everything will be a burden. Virtually any event will be filtered through your senses as being yet another cross for you to bear. If you are critical and constantly complain, any event will justify your perspective of being hard done by. If your attitude is fearful, everything will be a threat. Your senses will filter virtually any event as something that can hurt you or take something away from you. In all of these examples, your life will be extremely stressful and unhappy. Now imagine a positive, optimistic outlook. Your life will also have stress in it, but the way that stress is handled is completely different from the scenarios above. A wakeful, present, positive attitude will significantly reduce stress and contribute to finding joy and happiness in life. A person with this attitude has all the same things happen, like conflicts at work, relatives who are sick or dying, and financial pressures; however, how the person reacts to these things changes the entire situation.

You can adjust your attitude by making a conscious decision to do so. You can do this in any situation, in any one moment. Let's say that you get a difficult assignment at work. You have several choices. If you decide the assignment is a burden, you may lash out at your colleagues because they were not assigned the project. If you decide the assignment proves how hard done by you are, you will criticize your boss for giving it to you. If you decide the assignment is a threat to you, you will panic about how to get it done. However, if you decide that that the assignment is an opportunity for you to learn, you will enjoy the journey of doing the project.

We just took the exact same situation and demonstrated many different reactions. You are continually making choices about how you are going to perceive the things that happen around you. You are doing this moment-to-moment and day-by-day. The first step is to acknowledge that you do have the power to change your attitude, and through that, to change the outcome of a given situation. Practise adjusting your attitude in daily situations and experience the difference it makes to your sense of balance and contentment.

Reflection Exercise

Is there a situation at work that I can be more curious about?

_____

_____

_____

Is there a person at work I can stay more open to?

_____

_____

_____

What is one thing you learned at work this week?

_____

_____

_____

Take Care of your Body

The body you are in right now is the only one you're going to get. Imagine if the day you got your driver's licence you were also given the most beautiful car in the world. The only catch was that it would be the only car you would ever have. How would you treat it? Probably with a lot of loving care, which means the best fuel, oil changes, regular maintenance, and not driving it too hard. You would do everything you could to make sure that your prized car lasted as long as possible. Your body is also precious. It is the vehicle that allows you to see magical places, play with your kids, listen to music, hold hands, smell flowers, and taste a decadent dessert. Your body is looking for the same things that car is—care and respect. The only way you will succeed in caring for your body is to first decide that it matters to you. A good question to ask yourself is Why? Why is caring for myself important? Ask why before you move to how, where, when, and what. The answer to the why question may be to feel stronger, or to stay well as long as possible, or to be able to run around with your grandchildren when you are older. Answering the why question will help you stay motivated as you work through the other logistical questions of how, where, when, and what. The ongoing care of your body is a significant component to supporting a balanced and healthy life. In this regard, you can keep it really simple: Eat right, exercise, drink plenty of water, and get enough sleep. These are simple steps with profound results. Make a commitment to properly care for your one and only body.

Have a Personal Practice

As your life gets increasingly complicated with more responsibilities, the need to recharge yourself becomes more vital. That is why a great time to start a personal practice is right now. A personal practice is something you do alone, that has the combined effect of calming you down and lifting your spirit. This will mean different things to different people, but you will know what works for you. A personal practice might include gardening, playing a musical instrument, meditating, painting, or doing yoga. The personal practice that works for you will restore your energy and well-being and have the physiological benefits of keeping your mind calm and your body feeling better. I encourage you to find your personal practice and to carry it out daily or at least regularly enough that the benefits are maintained. For example, if playing the piano produces the benefits described, yet you play only during holidays, the benefits will not sustain themselves. I started meditating about ten years ago. I was horrible when I started. I actually ran away half way through my first meditation course. I went back and eventually got the hang of it (if one ever really does). Meditation has transformed my life and had the most significant impact on helping me be a better leader. Try to incorporate a daily personal practice into your life, even if only for a short time each day.

(i) *www.inspireyourcareer.com*

Nurture Your Soul

I have a group of women that I have known since our first year of university. We started a tradition of going away together one weekend every May. We recently celebrated the 25th anniversary of this event, called "Mayfest." Being with my friends during this weekend is profoundly uplifting. I look forward to it each year and am always sad when we have to say goodbye. We can all think of activities like this; the ones that nurture our soul. Perhaps you meet regularly with a group who shares a passion, like cars or playing bridge. Perhaps your family is a source of great joy and happiness for you. Having people in our lives who understand, support, and love us for who we are is a true gift. Being with them creates energy and vitality. Make and cherish the time you spend with the special people in your life. Your soul will be grateful.

Reflection Exercise
When do I feel uplifted?

What brings joy into my life?

Give Back

It is hard when you finish school, are neck deep in debt, and are trying to get your life on track to think about others. You are understandably absorbed with your job, your friends, and adjusting to your new career and life circumstances. But as soon as you can, try to find ways to give back to your community. Your community includes both your immediate community in your city or neighbourhood, and your global community including the environment. Giving back to your community can start with small things, like shovelling the sideway for the elderly lady who lives next door, running a race for charity, or volunteering at a soup kitchen. These are activities that will renew you. They give you a sense of purpose, accomplishment, and well-being, all of which reduce stress and help you achieve a more balanced life.

I have a friend who, in addition to running his own business and having a young family, organizes and leads volunteer trips to Guatemala. The volunteers install stoves, cement walls and floors, water filtration systems, and roofs to improve the living conditions of poor rural families. Having recently been on one of these life-altering trips, I was amazed at what my friend has accomplished. His leadership has resulted in the creation of infrastructure for entire villages. One person with a commitment to give back has affected the lives of thousands. You too can have this kind of impact. You are a citizen of your community, both locally and globally. You have a role to play in ensuring that these communities flourish, now and in the future. Do your part to give your time, your money, and your skills and enjoy the immeasurable rewards.

Inspire Your Career Tips

- Consciously decide what is important to you and shape your life accordingly.
- Stop doing things that do not add value to your life.
- Adjust your attitude to see situations in a positive light.
- Eat right, exercise, drink plenty of water and get enough sleep.
- Spend time with people who love, support, and uplift you.
- Give back to your local and global communities.

CHAPTER 14
Be the Inspiration

*"What lies behind us and what lies before us are tiny matters
compared to what lies within us."*
Ralph Waldo Emerson

What does it mean to inspire? The word itself comes from the Latin root *spirare*, which means to breathe. This is a very powerful image. It relates to life, to living, and to being alive. You can visualize inspiration as breathing life into yourself, into others, into the world. Inspiration comes from a place deep inside us, where the desire to use our gifts ignites and keeps our innermost passion burning. Keeping yourself open—heart, mind, and spirit—will help you get the best out of yourself, the best out of others, and the most out of your career. Everyone is drawn, naturally, to people who are inspiring. You can be inspiring too. As a matter of fact, you can start right now.

Be the Change

We all have within us an immense, limitless reserve of strength, compassion, and wisdom. These beautiful, powerful qualities have always been, and will always be accessible to us every day. Over time, because we are human, we cover up these qualities with fear, with anger, with jealousy, with rage, or with grief. Our strength, compassion, and wisdom start to diminish, not because they are not there, but because there are layers of other emotions on top of them. In your life, you will know the moments where, even briefly, you shed these layers and allow the power of who you are to shine. These moments are differentiated by feelings of intense happiness, contentment, love, peace, and joy. They may occur during a special event like a wedding or graduation, or when you are with a special person or in a special place, or when you accomplish something really important. We all know what these moments feel like. What most of us do not know, or perhaps do not believe, is that these moments are always available to us. We can choose to live our life without the layers that cover us up and drag us down. We have the power to draw on our own rich reserve every day. In order for you to be the change that you want to see in your workplace, you need to draw on this cache of strength, compassion, and wisdom.

In this book, we have discussed some of the ways that will help you do this, by knowing your blind spots, learning to reflect, and being better able to deal with conflict. These are all ways that will help you remove your negative layers at work and be more present and confident. By choosing to make conscious shifts at work, you can have a huge impact on your workplace. You can be the person who starts a different pattern, and a different way of doing things. We know that virtually any situation can be seen from different perspectives: some positive, some negative, some helpful, some not. Which will you choose? Every day at work you have choices, from moment to moment, hour to hour: You will choose how you treat another person; you will choose to listen or talk; and you will choose to be angry or calm. You will choose whether the layers of fear, aggression, and resentment cover up who you are, and the potential of who you could be. The idea is to think, speak, and act much more consciously.

If one of your layers is fear, for example, you may have difficulty handling conflict. At the first sign of conflict with a co-worker, your layer of fear will kick in to say, "I can't do this, sorry, I'm checking out." It is impossible for you to say what you want to say to the other person. Your courage is all covered up—but it does not have to be. You can alter your pattern. You do not have to accept that repetitive patterns in your life are permanent. You can consciously accept your fear, and simultaneously let your wisdom and courage shine. It is from this newly revealed place that you can have a profound impact on others and indeed be the change that you want to see in your workplace.

Which do you choose?

Your workplace is full of negativity, backstabbing, and hidden agendas. You hate it. You:
a) Lie low and try to stay out of the line of fire.

b) Find another job.
c) Draw on your strength and wisdom and start to deal
with people and issues differently.

A Lifelong Journey

In order to achieve your greatest potential, you need to commit to a lifelong journey of discovery and learning. This means embracing opportunities to learn more about who you are, learn more about others, and learn more about your world. Once you have this mindset, you will see that there are teachers everywhere. Your partner, your friends, your family, your co-workers, everyone becomes a rich source of insight, knowledge, and perspective. Having a mindset of discovery and learning gives you the open attitude to see, hear, and understand more. You can develop this mindset by being genuinely interested and inquisitive. Be curious about why situations are the way they are. Be inquisitive about understanding people. Be interested in what others say. Try to remember what it was like to be a child, experiencing the novelty, and pure wonder in everything. Having a sense of curiosity will help you stay open to new ideas, new ways of thinking, new opportunities, and new insights.

ⓘ *www.inspireyourcareer.com*

If we have the opposite attitude, one where we feel there is nothing more we need to learn, or that we are perfect the way we are, or that there is nothing others can teach us, we close down a creative part of our mind. In working hard to criticize or dismiss the wisdom that others can offer us through their words or actions, we shut down the opportunity to learn from that wisdom and, in turn, shut down the opportunity to offer our wisdom to others. In addition to being open to the wisdom of others, a lifelong journey of discovery and learning can be pursued through taking courses or reading books. Being open to discovery and learning means taking risks and trying new things, even if you are a little scared. It means being willing to try a different approach that someone suggests. It means getting out of your comfort zone and allowing new experiences in. Be committed to staying open to everything that you can learn and discover in life.

Reflection Exercise

What choices did I make at work this week that were positive?

_____

_____

_____

What choices did I make that were negative?

_____

_____

_____

What have I learned?

_____

_____

_____

Keep your Passion Alive

My martial arts *Sifu* (teacher) is passionate about what he does. He's in his fifties, and he is fit, dynamic, and enthusiastic every day. He is constantly encouraging people to stay healthy and learn and master the techniques of his craft. His genuine love for what he does makes him an inspiration to all his students. He is passionate about what he does and it shows. Others feel it instantly. Having passion for what you do is a path to happiness and a balanced life. As Confucius said, "Choose a job you love, and you will never have to work a day in your life." You may already be doing something you are passionate about in your career, which is fantastic. If you aren't, find out what it is that you are passionate about, nurture it, keep it alive, and find ways to bring passion into your day-to-day life.

In order to discover what you are passionate about, look at your soul, your core, and ask yourself, "What do I value?", "What do I love?" and "What inspires me?" Your answers to these questions are the building blocks of discovering what makes you feel enthusiastic and energized, and what stirs your passion. Perhaps you love to build things, or you are passionate about the environment or you adore working with children. Understanding what you are passionate about will lead you to opportunities and will guide you in making decisions about your work and your life. Once you have insight into what you are passionate about, you need to determine how it fits into your life. "Can it be part of my career, now or in the future?", "Can I find a job where I am able to do what I love?", "Will this be part of what I do on my own time?" You can keep your passion alive by finding others who are passionate about the same thing. Together, you create energy around whatever it is that fuels your passion. Your passion might turn into a great business or a hobby or your next job. You can also generate your own enthusiasm and energy around people, situations, and the things you do every day. Discover what you have to offer, what ignites your passion; bring it into your life and keep it alive.

Cultivate Gratitude

Cultivating gratitude shifts your perspective from one of scarcity and poverty, to one of abundance and richness. You start to see more options and more ways of doing things. Instead of having feelings of frustration and anger for what you have lost or do not have, you shift to feelings of appreciation for what you have gained and what you do have. One day you find yourself stewing over the fact that your colleague's work was recognized at the team meeting. You feel that you did just as much as she did and can't understand why you didn't get the same acknowledgement. The bitterness starts to build a wall of resentment and anger that isolates you from your colleague and boss. You build up the sense of scarcity and poverty, as if there is not enough appreciation to share. It is as if the recognition your colleague received takes away from the recognition that is available to you. In such situations, draw on your gratitude. In the same example, you can feel appreciative of what your colleague accomplished, congratulate her, and be thankful for the opportunity to see how someone else excelled and was recognized for her achievements. This approach builds the feeling of abundance and richness, and gives the impression that there is enough recognition for everyone and that everyone can excel. The next time a situation occurs, even if it is negative, ask, "What can I be grateful for in this situation?"

Cultivating gratitude is much easier if you consider the bigger picture. We are so blessed and privileged to live in a country with abundant food, water, electricity, stability, and peace, with money in our pocket and the potential to earn income. We could have been born into sickness and poverty or born in a country that is politically unstable or at war. Living where we are, right now, is a bigger prize than any lottery will ever pay. Be thankful. Cultivate a sense of gratitude in everything you do, in everything you say, and in everything you think. When you approach a situation from this perspective, its path will change. Resentment or anger can be transformed into new ways of seeing things. Let's assume you are almost finished a project and your boss gives you some additional information, which has an impact on what you are doing. Your reaction might be resentment or anger. "I can't believe I have to work this in, I was almost finished!" Try gratitude. By incorporating the information that you just received, the quality of your project will be significantly improved. The end result will be a report that better serves your team, the organization, and its clients. Cultivating gratitude is not easy, especially in a workplace where you often feel underappreciated, overworked, or stressed. As we said earlier, be the change. Cultivating gratitude is essential if you want to be the best person you can be in any situation.

Reflection Exercise
List five people or things that you are grateful for.

Be Courageous and Kind

One of the greatest things we have available to us every moment of the day is the heartfelt connection to others. We are always able to connect to the human condition with the knowledge that every other person is just like us, with the same fears, the same hopes, the same needs, and aspirations. I have travelled all over the world and am always struck by this fundamental truth. It does not matter where you go, people are the same everywhere. Yes, there are cultural and personality differences, but at the core, we are all one. Whether you are in Canada or Italy or Singapore or Argentina, whether you are in a tiny village or a major city, it is always the same. Parents want their children to be healthy, happy, and have more opportunities than they had. Young people want to socialize, be with their friends, and have fun. Children want to play, laugh, and feel secure. Business people want to cut the best deal, make some money, and be successful. Newlyweds profess their love to each other and plan their future together. Families gather together to share a meal and celebrate special moments. Old people gather together to tell stories and commiserate. We are all equal and we have a powerful connection to everyone around us and to everyone around the world.

When you can feel this connection to others, this commonality and unity, you will find a deep and unlimited source of courage and kindness. You are courageous because you see the powerful connection you have to everyone and everything. Seeing your equal place in this world gives you confidence and allows you to overcome your fears. You are kind because you see the beauty and magic in everything it surrounds you, it engulfs you. When you can be courageous and kind, fearless and compassionate, strong and vulnerable, you draw out your greatest human qualities. You become a natural, inspiring leader.

Inspire Your Career Tips

- Be the change in your workplace.
- Commit to lifelong learning and personal growth.
- Discover what stirs your passion and ignite it.
- Be thankful for everything and everyone in your life.
- Be a natural, inspiring leader.

References

Chapter 1
1. Boutin, C. 2006. Snap judgments decide a face's character, psychologist finds.
   http://www.princeton.edu/main/news/archive/S15/62/69K40/index.xml?section=topstories

Chapter 3
2. George, B., P. Sims, A.N. McLean, and D. Mayer. Feb 2007. "Discovering your Authentic Leadership." *Harvard Business Review.*
3. Liker, J. 2004. *The Toyota Way.* New York: McGraw-Hill.
4. Arbinger Institute. 2002. *Leadership and Self Deception: Getting Out of the Box.* San Francisco: Berrett-Koehler Publishers.

Chapter 5
5. Paul, R., Binker, A., Jensen, K. and Kreklau, H. 1990. *Critical Thinking Handbook: A Guide for Remodelling Lesson Plans in Language Arts, Social Studies, and Science.* Rohnert Park: Foundation for Critical Thinking.

Chapter 6
6. Wanberg, C.R., E.T. Welsh and S.A. Hexlett. 2003. "Mentoring research: A review and dynamic process model." *Research in Personnel and Human Resources Management*, Vol 22. Greenwich, CT: JAI Press.
7. Henien, A. and F. Morissette. 2007. *Made in Canada Leadership: Wisdom from the Nation's Best and Brightest on the Art and Practice of Leadership.* Mississauga: John Wiley & Sons.

Chapter 7
8. Catalyst. 2009. Women CEOs of the Fortune 1000. *http://www.catalyst.org/publication/322/women-ceos-of-the-fortune-1000*

Catalyst. 2009. 2009 Catalyst Census: Fortune 500 Women Board Directors. *http://www.catalyst.org/publication/357/2009-catalyst-census-fortune-500-women-board-directors*

Catalyst. 2009. Australia, Canada, South Africa & United States. *http://www.catalyst.org/publication/239/australia-canada-south-africa-united-states*

Index